Bermuda Triangle

Unexplained Disappearances Beneath the Waves

(A True Story of Strange Events From the Bermuda Triangle)

Connie Dennis

Published By **Regina Loviusher**

Connie Dennis

All Rights Reserved

Bermuda Triangle: Unexplained Disappearances Beneath the Waves (A True Story of Strange Events From the Bermuda Triangle)

ISBN 978-1-77485-517-1

No part of this guidebook shall be reproduced in any form without permission in writing from the publisher except in the case of brief quotations embodied in critical articles or reviews.

Legal & Disclaimer

The information contained in this ebook is not designed to replace or take the place of any form of medicine or professional medical advice. The information in this ebook has been provided for educational & entertainment purposes only.

The information contained in this book has been compiled from sources deemed reliable, and it is accurate to the best of the Author's knowledge; however, the Author cannot guarantee its accuracy and validity and cannot be held liable for any errors or omissions. Changes are periodically made to this book. You must consult your doctor or get professional medical advice before using any of the suggested remedies, techniques, or information in this book.

Upon using the information contained in this book, you agree to hold harmless the Author from and against any damages, costs, and expenses, including any legal fees potentially resulting from the application of any of the information provided by this guide. This disclaimer applies to any damages or injury caused by the use and application, whether directly or indirectly, of any advice or information presented, whether for breach of contract, tort, negligence, personal injury, criminal intent, or under any other cause of action.

You agree to accept all risks of using the information presented inside this book. You need to consult a professional medical practitioner in order to ensure you are both able and healthy enough to participate in this program.

Table of Contents

Introduction 1

Chapter 1: What Exactly Is The Bermuda Triangle? 2

Chapter 2: What Is The Truth Lies?.39

Chapter 3: Similar Paranormal Phenomena 44

Chapter 4: Theories, And Natural Explanations 54

Chapter 5: Definition Of The Crystal Pyramids..59

Chapter 6: A Few Explanations Are Scientifically Based, Even Or At Least, In The Evidence 68

Chapter 7: The History And Mystery Of The Bermuda Triangle..............100

Chapter 8: Bermuda Triangle Theories And Counter-Theories....127

Chapter 9: Investigation 148

Chapter 10: Gas Explosions In Bermuda Triangle 169

Conclusion 184

Introduction

The Bermuda Triangle is a region located in the western region of the North Atlantic Ocean in which planes, ships and individuals are said to have mysteriously disappeared.

Fig . 1.1.1: The map illustrates where the Bermuda Triangle is located in general famous Bermuda Triangle. For many years the Atlantic Ocean's fabled Bermuda Triangle has captured the imagination of mankind with the mysterious disappearances of planes, ships and even people.

There is speculation that unidentified and unidentified forces are responsible for the mysterious disappearances, like extraterrestrials taking human beings for research and an influence from the lost continent of Atlantis and vortices that pull objects into different dimensions as well as other wacky theories.

Chapter 1: What Exactly Is The Bermuda Triangle?

The Bermuda Triangle is commonly regarded as one of the most significant mysteries of our time But what exactly is it?

The Triangle is also referred to also as Devil's Triangle is a part of the western part of the North Atlantic Ocean. The area is delineated by imaginary lines that run from Florida to Bermuda, the island of Bermuda and then on towards Puerto Rico, and lastly returning to Florida making a triangular shape.

The mystery stems from numerous ships and aircraft which mysteriously vanished inside the Triangle in strange circumstances.

This phenomenon can lead to many theories as well as hypotheses and explanations. They are ranging from the superstitious and religious to the mundane and scientific.

However, the records about Bermuda Triangle events are often filled with inaccurate facts, misleading reports, and fabricated stories. Research into the region is usually conducted with a bias toward a particular view, resulting in an unjustified dismissal of data or the acceptance of inaccuracy-based data, which is later asserted as fact.

You may be thinking, "How did the Triangle get its name?" Well, it's difficult to determine without falling into a trap. However, let's attempt to figure out the source!

The history of the Bermuda Triangle

The underlying mythology is as hazy as the myth itself but , in a way that's part of the appeal! Let's go back to the beginning of the myth.

The Origin

A variety of theories about the phenomenon were raised before an "formal" description of the triangle in 1964. One of them was made in the words of none but Christopher Columbus, who reported that his ships had irregular readings of the compass when sailing through the Sargasso Sea. They also saw mysterious light sources on the horizon on the 11th of October 1492. These events remain unsolved.

The Spark

The genesis of this legend occurred conceived in 1950, thanks to an article written in 1950 by Edward Van Winkle Jones in The Miami Herald. The article is regarded as the first directly referring to Bermuda Triangle. Bermuda Triangle.

Jones has cited a variety of instances, including the 5th December 1945 disappearance Flight 19, a training flight with five US Navy TBM Avenger torpedo bombers that never made it back to their home base.

The most shocking element of the disappearance was the fact that the aircraft used to search and rescue that was deployed to search for the plane was also missing. Since no reason has been definitively established the theories surrounding what happened are all based on speculation.

Jones also mentioned the disappearance of commercial airlines Star Tiger as well as Star Ariel in 1948 and 1949, respectively. Star Tiger was traveling from the Azores to Bermuda and Star Ariel was traveling from the Azores in the Azores to Kingston, Jamaica.

In both instances both instances, the planes appeared to be operating above their capabilities, and these incidents could be due to technical problems, but not necessarily a cause of any relief to the families of the passengers on the aircraft.

The Mystery

George X. Sand contributed to the myth two years after Jones's piece.

For Fate publication, the author wrote an article titled "Sea The Mystery Behind Our Door" where he described a string of disappearances with no trace that occurred in what was described as the "watery triangle bordered roughly with Florida, Bermuda, and Puerto Rico." He clearly laid the groundwork for what we know today is"the Bermuda Triangle.

Similar to Jones, Sand cited the notorious Flight 19. Sand also reported a number of other disappearances. One of them was that of Sandra the tramp, a square-cut steamer that was heading to Georgia towards Puerto Cabello, Venezuela. The steamer's heavy weight vanished in the process which led to the investigation being categorized unsolved "unsolved" after a few days of unsuccessful investigation.

Sand also reported his disappearance Albert Snider, an American jockey. In the search to find Snider was a labor of at least 800 people, however, despite all efforts, they could not find his skiff, tangled in the mangroves on an unknown island. It was searched for hours but could not find any conclusive evidence of what transpired to Snider on the 5th of March 1948.

Another disappeared the occurred in the same year. On the 28th of December the DC-3 transportation plane headed towards Miami coming from San Juan, Puerto Rico. Everything appeared to be well even the weather looked pleasant but the plane simply... went missing. The plane was never found and no trace of it has been found as of yet.

The Paranormal

With the ever-growing desire for answers to the mystery disappearances seemed natural to believe that they were caused by the supernatural or... not quite natural. In his book from 1955, The Case for the UFO, M.K. Jessup employed a number of stories previously mentioned to make a case for alien life forms from the universe. Jessup's viewpoint was amplified by the work of Donald E. Keyhoe's The Flying Saucer Conspiracy, also published in 1955 and Frank Edwards' Stranger Than Science (1959).

"Bermuda Triangle." The phrase "Bermuda Triangle" was coined in 1964 by Vincent H. Gaddis in his article "The Deadly Bermuda Triangle" for the magazine Argosy. Gaddis established the boundaries of the Bermuda Triangle more precisely than Sand by naming its vertex boundaries in the form of Miami, Puerto Rico, and Bermuda.

Gaddis's report was a bit exaggerated in that he claimed over 1,000 people had been lost in the region. However, Jones's piece in 1950 was based on 135 deaths. But the assumption that there was some sort of "pattern of odd incidents" and "in the series of catastrophes" there was not one body that was located, was certainly not untrue. The story clearly demonstrated an incredibly terrifying truth that no matter how sophisticated our technology or deep our investigations it is possible to vanish completely and completely without a trace.

The fascination with the Triangle began to take off in the first decade of the 1970s. In the next few years, every well-known "paranormal" or "true mystery" book had an entire section (or greater) about Bermuda Triangle "deadly" Bermuda Triangle, but you can also find it with various names, such as"Devil's Triangle, "Devil's Triangle" or the "Hoodoo Sea."

There are a variety of printed books on the subject that we can find Invisible Residents, by Ivan T. Sanderson and released in 1970. The book discusses in detail the Bermuda

Triangle as evidence of an advanced, intelligent and technologically sophisticated underwater civilization.

Limbo of the Lost, written by John Wallace Spencer, was released in 1969 and was able to boast an enormous readership by the year 1973.

The most significant of all is the self-titled The Bermuda Triangle, a bestseller written by Charles Berlitz and J. Manson Valentine and released in 1974. The book sent Triangle fever to the top of the charts.

The Debunking

For readers who were critical and attentive it was evident that the writers were copying each other's work. There was the evidence of any original research and so-called chroniclers of the Triangle were quickly discredited.

In the wake of the record-breaking popularity of the books of 1974 The Devil's Triangle, by Richard Winer, and No Earthly Explanation by John Wallace Spencer, who seemed to be hoping to make a name for himself in the subject matter--Larry Kusche who was library librarian from Arizona State University, conducted his own research, and then published an article that dealt the ultimate blow to what he described as"a "manufactured crime."

The piece that was in question, titled The Bermuda Triangle Mystery: Solved The work was the result of archival research that was thorough that was often ignored by the previous authors. Kusche used the weather records, official reports from the investigation agencies, newspaper reports as well as a myriad of additional documents to determine if that the "Bermuda Triangle writing" was fair to the evidence.

Kusche found that earlier writers were a bit sloppy in this respect, and even dirty. For example, the conditions which were reported in the books as "calm oceans" in the book were actually storms that were raging and ships gone "without any trace" were long ago discovered; and finally, "ominous disappearances" were entirely normal sinking disasters.

In addition to denying the notion of claims of a Bermuda Triangle mystery, a spokesperson on behalf of Lloyd's of London wrote a letter to the editor of the magazine Fate, Mary Margaret Fuller. He said that according to Lloyd's documents there were 428 ships were reported missing around the world between

1955 and 1975. The problem was that Lloyd's found no proof that suggests that the Bermuda Triangle had experienced more loss than any other place. The letter was accepted by the US Coastguard based on their computerized documents of the Atlantic that go back as far as 1958.

In the wake of these protests, the Bermuda Triangle proponents had to present a convincing defense in order to have any credibility at all. But they reacted to the facts with a mute silence. It's no surprise that it did not inspire confidence among the population that Bermuda Triangle represented an authentic anomaly.

There's plenty of research experts who say that "skeptics" aren't willing to unravel the mystery. But, their claims are a joke when compared to some facts like the numerous "Bermuda Triangle disappearances" which didn't really occur in the Bermuda Triangle.

Skeptics, on other hand, assert that no research to date has yielded any evidence of any peculiarity or any other explanation for disappearances. According to them they don't need an assessment of strength between the two sides, since explanations, including scientific ones, aren't required.

In a way the most intriguing part is the way in which it began instead of the fact that it's actually happening.

The Legacy

Even now, more than fifty years later, the Bermuda Triangle occasionally resurfaces in the tabloids. While the old legend has been reduced to the margins of history but its influence on popular culture is undeniable.

The Triangle remains the focus of a recurrent conflict between pseudoscientific and scientific debate, although it's the comparatively smaller number of people. Beyond that, the diverse aspects in the story have influenced numerous television shows, movies books, video games.

Timeless classics like the first Scooby-Doo cartoon as well as the sci-fi show X-Files have included in the Bermuda Triangle.

Capcom's video game Dark Void features a protagonist who is transported to another dimension as she travels throughout in the Bermuda Triangle.

Arthur Rankin Jr. wrote and directed his own Bermuda Triangle-themed television film in the year 1978. The co-production between Japan and America was shot at the shores of Bermuda. The film follows the tale of an abandoned college student who returns to Bermuda in search of the cause of his father's death many years before.

The Bermuda Triangle craze left its impression. It doesn't matter if, like the majority of people, you take the skeptical viewpoint or decide to take a stand in the paranormal versus scientific debate it's likely that you've heard of the Bermuda Triangle in the past. This was an integral part of the Zeitgeist of the past and is an excellent illustration how religion is paired with technology. It's possibly one of the very last examples we will encounter in this era of advancements in science and the ubiquitous collection of data.

Information about Bermuda Triangle Bermuda Triangle

1. The Bermuda Triangle's Area Is Not properly defined.

The questionable management of the mythology has created a baffling circumstance: the Triangle's region isn't properly defined. Researchers, journalists and self-appointed experts frequently differ with Vincent Gaddis's initial description of the vertex boundaries of Bermuda Triangle as Miami, San Juan, and Bermuda. Later journalists and writers have proposed different boundaries, and the area can vary between 500,000 and 1.510,000 sq miles.

This is a significant obstacle for Bermuda Triangle's paranormal advocates since skeptics could conveniently point out that the majority of the "Bermuda Triangle disappearances" didn't occur within the boundaries of the Triangle in the way they define it.

2. Bermuda Triangle Bermuda Triangle Doesn't Like Compasses

Indeed! It is one of the two locations on Earth where a compass is pointed not in the direction of magnetic north, but rather towards the true north.

This might require an explanation for those who aren't acquainted with navigation on the sea. Actually there are many different "norths" however we need only to comprehend two of them in this article:

True North The meridians meet at the northern hemisphere also known as it is the North Pole. You can see that real south refers to the opposite of true north, The South Pole.

Magnetic North: Found at Ellesmere Island in Northern Canada. The magnetic lines that run north cross the Earth. A compass needle aligns itself with the field magnetic of our planet and thus it (usually) will point toward magnetic north.

Sailors have been aware of the difference between magnetic and true north since the invention of the compass and they have always taken into account this information to their navigation. The variance between the two is known as magnetic variation, or magnetic declination. it is believed that the US Coast Guard was only affirming the obvious when it stated it was "if this compass error or error isn't compensated by the navigator, they might end up off direction and in serious trouble."

The truth is that Bermuda Triangle has an uncommon magnetic declination isn't the reason for the absence of. Magnetic variation has been extensively studied, and even a skilled navigator (or even a beginner) is aware of the compass variations within the region as a matter of fact. The majority of them would not reach their destinations anyplace in the world without it!

3. Bermuda Triangle is Not Officially Recognized. Bermuda Triangle is Not Officially Recognized

Although most people are aware of the Triangle but there's no official information about it. The Triangle isn't identified by maps; it's an area of water we've come to call Bermuda Triangle. Bermuda Triangle. Anything that occurs within this Bermuda Triangle is simply something that takes place within the boundaries that is defined by three imaginary vertices. as mentioned that these vertices are different based on the person who's imagine.

4. The Bermuda Triangle's weather is extremely wild.

Really, don't allow a professional writer to tell you that the weather in the Triangle is quiet! The Triangle region, as well as being a popular destination for hurricanes, is frequently subject to violent storms that strike suddenly and other weather events that are unexpected. Although they usually disappear quickly, their severity can cause serious navigational issues.

5. Its Triangle Topography of Bermuda's Triangle Topography is Scary

Imagine what could be the consequences if you were to fall into an ocean trench. And then... you kept... sliding...

The topography under the water of the Bermuda Triangle is inconsistent, to put it in a mild way it varies from gentle sloped continental shelves to deep ocean trenches. In fact there are some of the world's deepest trenches can be found in this region. In the Puerto Rico Trench has an average depth of less than five miles and can reach 5.3 miles at its highest!

If a plane, or a ship is swept away by the trench or one in the Bermuda Triangle trenches, recovery of the wreckage would effectively be impossible. The safest distance at which we are able to breathe air is around 200 feet. Utilizing special equipment, we can reach anywhere between 1,600 to 2,600 feet below the surface. However, after 1,600 feet, it's an opportunity to gamble. It's only about a half mile. Then let it take in...

6. The Bermuda Triangle's currents are turbulent

The sinking of a bottomless, watery grave isn't all it takes for a ship to go under from the Bermuda Triangle. There are other swift turbulent currents. The Triangle is situated in the Gulf Stream, which moves extremely fast, often exceeding five knots in certain regions.

These currents can easily send sailors off course for miles. Furthermore, in case of wreck all debris could be swiftly swept by the currents. This is the reason for the mysterious nature of some disappearances.

7. The United States has a Laboratory in the Bermuda Triangle

For more specific information to be precise, the US laboratory can be found at Andros Island in the Bahamas.

The facility is high-tech and has many different missions connected to simulation of undersea warfare. Its mission is to establish an environment for polishing and sustaining the capabilities for the US Navy. In this regard it conducts tasks like testing the capability of simulation, testing, evaluation and research.

The character of the laboratory together with its area and the eerie absence of information about what it is have led to several unanswered questions. The brief story however, appears to suggest that the Navy utilizes the space of the ocean for testing submarines and other underwater weapons.

8. In the Bermuda Triangle's Ocean Floor traps Methane Gas

The existence of huge quantities of methane gas that are trapped on the bottom of oceans isn't dangerous... except if it is released.

The gas is produced by decomposing sea creatures; the sediment is a home for bacteria that produce methane while they eat dead animals. Methane accumulated in the form of a methane ice with a high concentration known as gas hydrates. The ice layer in the process traps methane gas and when the gas pockets rupture and the gas rises into a turbulent column that drastically reduces the density that the liquid.

A vessel that is located within the vicinity of the blowout could sink rapidly. The extent to which this took place in the Bermuda Triangle remains unknown.

9. The Bermuda Triangle Experiences a lot of Traffic

In the past, there has been lots of trade across in the Caribbean from the Caribbean to Europe. In the past, ships carried tobacco, sugar and rum. Today, in modern times, they transport containers that are filled with anything you can imagine. In reality Bermuda Triangle Bermuda Triangle is one of the most traveled shipping routes in the world.

The expense of alternative routes makes staying clear of the Triangle difficult, and many sailors aren't scared of it, perhaps because they've experienced it so many times. Consider this Do you feel scared of driving to work?

The more frequent travel may be the cause of the seemingly high amount of disappearances that occur in the Bermuda Triangle. The numbers are large in the sense of absolute however, it's normal to expect that regions that have less traffic will see less disappearances.

Background information on the Bermuda Triangle

There are many theories about the events that are taking place in the legend-making Bermuda Triangle. The theories originate from sailors and mariners, research and academics, historians, journalists, UFO experts, and paranormal fans, and often, out-and-out charlatans.

The basis of these theories vary widely as well they are not all as simple and scientifically sound as the idea concerning methane gas blowouts while others are so absurd and speculative that they claim that under in the Bermuda Triangle lies the lost city of Atlantis.

Even if it's not your intention to purchase any of these stories but reading them will surely be an enjoyable experience. Let's take a look at some of the more well-known explanations, divided into the paranormal and scientific. Maybe one of them appeals to you!

Scientific Theories

Hexagonal Clouds

The number of deaths which have occurred within the Bermuda Triangle is a hot subject. Some sources claim that more than 1,000 deaths have occurred in the past 45 years; some claim it's closer to 1,000; and some claim that it doesn't reach 800. However you cut it, plenty of people have been killed there, and ships as well as aircrafts are certainly lost.

The most common explanations for this we have factors like the strength of the Gulf Stream, the erratic weather, and even the hazardous topography. But, meteorologists have recently come up with a new hypothesis to explain the alleged mysteries of the Bermuda Triangle.

The researchers have discovered a peculiar pattern in the clouds of the region The hexagonal pattern is a surprise!

In addition to their unique shape, these clouds are also capable of generating violent 170-miles-per-hour "air explosions"! These violent gales might be at the root of some of the trouble that occurs in the region.

The claim is based in images from the NASA satellite. Researchers concluded that hexagonal clouds could grow to be up to between 20 and 55 miles in size and that the waves within the air bombs may be upwards of 45 feet.

The Science Channel's What on Earth, Randy Cerveny who is Professor of Geographic Sciences of Arizona State University, stated that the images are "really strange" because skies have sharp edges. This is very unusual because clouds are very vastly randomly distributed in the way they are.

The clouds release blasts of air which bombard everything in between the clouds and the ocean. Therefore, anything within the range that an air blast can easily be thrown from the sky and tossed overboard, or drowned.

Methane Hydrates

The US Geological Survey has discovered massive deposits of methane Hydrates off in the southeast coast part of the United States.

It is among the most well-known globally, in fact.

These methane gas levels, located thousands of feet below the seafloor, are usually dormant. However, occasional eruptions can result in violent releases of gas which result in significant reductions in the water's density.

When the density decreases, the water turns frothy and ineffective at providing the buoyancy required for keeping a ship on its feet. In this situation the ship will simply sink without warning. With the power of the Gulf Stream, a ship could sink by the ocean, carried miles from its planned route, and later covered in sediment.

In a way it is comparable to the air bombs. While an air bomb could smash a ship into waters from the top, methane-hydrate eruption could replace the water beneath the ship's bottom by gas-filled columns that allows the ship to sink.

Don't take it as a given that these eruptions be limited to vessels. In the case of particularly intense eruptions the atmosphere above could be saturated with methane gas which could cause turbulence that could cause aircraft crashes.

Another possible, yet unlikely incident related to methane-rich hydrates is the creation of huge bubbles in the sea floor - as in larger than a ship's bubbles. They would then break off and then ascend towards the surface. Because of the lower tension, the bubbles would continue expanding until they reached the surface. If a vessel happens to come through during this time it would explode the bubble. The empty inside of the bubble would then engulf the entire ship, and bring it to its lowest point. The gas in the bubbles will be extremely hot, and the blowout may result in fires, possibly in aircrafts that fly above.

Sea Attrition

In a way, the theory of sea attrition is comparable in some ways to the Skeptics' belief which claims that "there's nothing mysterious" about Bermuda Triangle. Bermuda Triangle. But it's not the same because it acknowledges the uniqueness of the region. It's a reference to a mix of three dangers.

First, the underwater terrain of Bermuda Triangle is very wild. The patterns are unique and can crop up without warning. In one instance you're sailing along the gentle slope, then within the next, you're facing an abrupt drop of miles. Naturally should a plane or a vessel was to fall into an abyss, there would be nothing to be salvaged, since it's a deep depth that's not yet accessible to the human race.

The climate that occurs in the Bermuda Triangle area is very unstable. The calm waves that provide a nice breeze can swiftly give way to a storm of high intensity with massive waves, referred to in the field as "freak waves." Unprepared navigators as well as his vessel may be caught in a storms, literally. The weather shifts can be so rapid that satellites are unable to effectively capture them, however they're strong enough to cause destruction to smaller aircrafts or ships. In addition, you can add waterspouts and hurricanes (basically an ocean tornado that hurls water up to a distance of thousands of feet in the sky) and you've got very hazardous weather.

The third is The Sargasso Sea. It's a bizarre area especially for Bermuda Triangle. The Sargasso Sea isn't surrounded by shores. Instead, it's bordered by ocean currents from all sides. In the Age of Sail, this sea snared many ships due to its weak winds and dense sargassum seaweed.

The steady, calm conditions for weather in the Sargasso Sea might sound enticing but it's not the case! Sailboats without a steady breeze may be almost still in the ocean. As if that weren't enough of a barrier in the direction of forward motion If a vessel is moving slow is likely to become stuck in the seaweed thick that is characteristic of the Sargasso Sea.

There's an interesting tale about this which involves Spanish sailors during the period of colonization of New World. When their vessels became trapped for weeks, they were forced take difficult choices to ensure their safety. One of the options was to throw their horses into the sea to conserve drinking water. Because of this, it is said that the Sargasso Sea has also been referred to for its Horse Latitudes.

The three factors together create an extremely dangerous circumstance for seafarers. Given the number of similar-looking islands within the region it is easy for a captain to make the wrong path. If this happened and the severe storm conditions made trip more dangerous What could happen to the vessel? If it was going to the wrong way the vessel could be left with no fuel to get to the land. If the ship were to sink at sea level in Sargasso Sea the only alternative could be disaster.

With the advancement of technology, this is all less likely now However, the main point remains: Attrition is not a joke!

There is no mystery at All

It takes only some scientists to disprove over 70 years of incessant speculations. Many skeptical scientists claim that Bermuda Triangle solved. Bermuda Triangle mystery solved by declaring that there was never any mystery at all in the beginning.

What is their claim to this? They've got a few reasons that they believe provide a reason why the events in the Bermuda Triangle aren't as shocking as many people make them appear. They say the primary reason for this series of disappearances has to do with human error paired with weather conditions that are bad. Both occur all over the world.

They claim that the entire mystery was born of lying and exaggerations, expertly and purposefully written by professional writers or scammers, as some claim.

The most important reason for the theory of due to the dimensions of the area (we're talking approximately around 270,000 square kilometers at minimum) and the high volume of speed of travel, accidents are sure to occur. Although the number of deaths in the Triangle may be more significant in numbers but it's no different as any other area around the globe on a per-cent basis.

One of the most prominent advocates of the idea that the mystery isn't a mystery in the first place are Karl Kruszelnicki, an Australian scientist who is a collaborator at Sydney University. He has dissected the notorious incident in Flight 19 to prove that the Triangle authors exaggerated their tales in order to promote their books.

In his study, Kruszelnicki refutes Vincent Gaddis's article "The Deadly Bermuda Triangle" by noting that although Gaddis claimed that the group "vanished under ideal conditions for flight" however the weather was not ideal. There were large 50-foot waves in the region.

He also reveals certain details Gaddis did not feel it was appropriate to include. Most notable is the lack of experience of pilots, as well as the lack of competence of their leader, Lieutenant. Charles Taylor. Kruszelnicki exposes how Lieutenant. Taylor "arrived with a hangover, departed without any watch, and also had a the habit of wandering off and then reversing his aircraft."

To prove this Kruszelnicki references radio transcripts that were recorded prior to the disappearance. They indicate that Taylor discovered a glitch in his compass (a characteristic of the region) and stated that he was in his destination in the Florida Keys. According to ground personnel it appears that the was located above an island located in the Bahamas at the time of the incident.

The transcripts indicate that Taylor also instructed all the pilots in his group to go west further into the Atlantic rather than fly to the east towards the mainland.

The water in the area is deep enough that it would be nearly impossible to find sunken bodies or planes, even today.

To their credit, Lloyd's of London have stated that everything that transpires within the Bermuda Triangle happens at the same pace as it happens everywhere and everywhere else since they wrote to Fate in the year 1975.

Paranormal Theories

The Lost City of Atlantis

You're reading it right. This theory is based upon the mythical city of Atlantis. When you've stopped laughing about the notion we should take a second to look it up.

It is believed that the mythical city was awash with advanced technology as well as some that were abandoned. According to the Atlantis idea of the Bermuda Triangle centers on underwater rock formations referred to by Bimini Road. Bimini Road.

Edgar Cayce, an American Christian mystic who was born in 1877, was believed to have prophesied that the city Atlantis was to come to light in the near future. In 1968, 23 years following his death, scientists discovered stones as well as other odd structures near the shore from Bimini Island in the Bahamas.

They concluded that they were natural phenomena, however Cayce's theories convinced many. The people who believe that these stones have been perfectly arranged that they be the walls and roads of Atlantis. There is no evidence to support this assertion however it shouldn't be dismissed without a doubt without the presence of a scientifically conclusive explanation of the odd patterns.

Sonar images taken in early 2001 close to Cuba reveal geometrically symmetrical stone structures that look like an underwater urban complex. Without further evidence this is an incredible discovery that isn't able to be tied into any sort of theory, but it certainly helped the advocates of theories like the Atlantis theory!

Let's return to the question How is the city that was never found in Atlantis connected to the alleged supernatural disappearances of the Bermuda Triangle?

The legend relates to particular, extremely powerful energy crystals that were crucial in the urban area. The power they produced could be used to create an "death radiation." The advocates of the theory claim that a lot disappearances may be a result of energy discharges which either damaged navigational devices or destroyed ships and airplanes themselves.

The sea is full mysteries! Numerous underwater expeditions conducted in the waters of the Bahamas have revealed bizarre patterns, like an entirely smooth, granite-like ocean floor and structures that appear human-made. However, despite these intriguing discoveries there are no energy crystals or similar to them, have been discovered so far.

Aliens

It's difficult to decide which is more likely aliens abducting ships and planes from precisely within the Bermuda Triangle, or energy crystals from the mythical city of Atlantis smashing them to pieces. Let's dive into this idea!

We must first comprehend the exact time frame in the time that the five military aircrafts from Flight 19 lost contact on December 5th 1945. Superstition and speculation were slowly being replaced by scientifically-backed theories and facts, but this particular event couldn't be resolved in that manner. The conspiracy theorists were left to develop whatever theories they liked.

The person who was the one to help them gain a place to stand in the field was Charles Berlitz, author of the best-selling The Bermuda Triangle. Berlitz wrote that, considering the absence of a rationally plausible theory, "independent researchers" might be able to legitimately consider "extraordinary" theories. Then he addressed "exceptions to the natural law" and the possibility of disappearances being manipulated by "entities that originate from outer or inner space."

Of course, this notion is a pure speculation, but the theorists took a leap of faith on an unconfirmed factual event: the alleged UFO glimpse of Christopher Columbus as he sailed through the Sargasso Sea.

As we mentioned earlier the explorer who stumbled upon the Americas in 1492 saw unidentifiable lights at the horizon when traveling through the waters of Sargasso Sea. To be exact it was noted in his journal that he saw a bright light that looked like "the glowing light of a candle." candle that was moving up and down."

The exact details of what Columbus and his crew witnessed is almost impossible to discuss right today... But then wouldn't that be the ultimate definition of UFOs? UFO?

A majority of modern conspiracy theorists believe that the disappearances of airplanes be due to an "hole that is in the air" which aircrafts can go through but not leave. Others suggest that aircrafts and ships are being taken by aliens.

"The Souls of Slaves"

It's actually an extremely plausible supernatural explanations, provided that it's not an exaggeration. This theory puts the Bermuda Triangle's disappearances, deaths and deaths on the curse. The theory was developed in the work of Kenneth McAll, a psychiatrist at Brook Lyndhurst, an independent research and strategy consulting.

McAll believes that the region could be haunted by the spirits of the numerous African slaves taken into the ocean during their journey to America during the early 18th century.

In his book from 1989, Healing the Haunted, McAll describes his bizarre experiences when sailing through the water of the Triangle. McAll claims he heard an unending sound like mournful singing. The waters were calm and the atmosphere pleasant and warm, and McAll dismissed the sound as music emanating from the cabins of the crew.

The noise continued but it continued to play through the night. McAll inquired about the sound, and they were as confused as McAll was.

It sparked a sense of fear and fascination that made him want to know more about the oceans themselves. He discovered that in the period of 18th-century, violent and uncaring British captains of the sea had defrauded insurance companies by throwing African slaves to the ocean, and letting them drown to claim on the victims.

So far, we've discussed the mythology of ancient times flying saucers, flying nymphs and ghosts that are vengeful. So , what's next? ...?

Electronic Fog

What do you mean by electronic fog is it?

The theory, formulated by Robert MacGregor along with Bruce Gernon in their 2005 book The Fog, claims that the myriad of mysterious and unsolved disappearances and events that occur in Bermuda Triangle Bermuda Triangle are due to the formation of a tunnel-like cortex from what appears to be clouds, an electronic fog.

According to Gernon Gernon, the two of them witnessed the phenomenon in person while flying his Bonanza A36 over the Bahamas. They were flying towards Bimini when they came across it.

Gernon states how the wings scampered along the edges of the tunnel while they were passing and the plane's electrical and magnetic equipment, including navigational equipment, malfunctioned. He observed the magnetic compass was spinning quickly and mysteriously.

As the plane of Gernon neared the close of the tunnel, Gernon and his father hoped to be greeted by the bright blue sky once more. But instead, they confronted by a terrifying view of a dull , grayish white that spanned to several miles. There was no sky, ocean or the familiar the horizon.

However, the equipment was working again after a flight of 34 minutes, an amount that was apparently confirmed by the clocks on board, they finally reached Miami Beach.

The average flight time is 75 minutes.

MacGregor and Gernon strongly believe that the "electronic fog" that Gernon was able to experience is at fault for the notorious disappearances of the region like the case from Flight 19.

Vortices

They are more popularly referred to as the vile vortices. Invisible Residents author Ivan T. Sanderson invented the term, which is a reference to mysterious sites that have disappearances as well as other mysterious events. In these locations is Bermuda Triangle. Bermuda Triangle.

According to Ivan Ivan, there are twelve vortices located along specific areas of high latitude. Five of them are located on the same latitude southern hemisphere of the Equator. other five are at the same latitude north and last two are located between the south and north poles.

The concept of paranormal phenomena that follow geometric patterns isn't new in and of itself. It is extensively explored by the author of Anti-gravity and the World Grid which was first published in 1987.

The vortices that have been identified are as follows:

* Bermuda Triangle (of course)
* Algerian Megaliths (South of Timbuktu, Mali)
* Indus Valley (Mohenjo-daro, Pakistan)
* Hamakulia Volcano (East of Hawaii)
* Devil's Sea (South of Japan)
* Anomaly in the South Atlantic
* Wharton Basin (northeastern Indian Ocean)
* Easter Island Megaliths
* East of Rio de Janeiro
* Loyalty Islands (New Caledonia)
* North Pole
* South Pole

A variety of theories have emerged to explain the presumed connection between the geography and mysterious happenings. Some suggest that the vortices are connected to the "ley lines" or "ley lines"--apparent geocentric alignments of landforms with ancient spiritual significance, typically embellished with structures made by humans. Some believe that there is some sort of "electromagnetic distortion" in these areas Some believe in the existence of "subtle energies in matter."

Addendum

There are numerous theories of the supernatural that explain Bermuda Triangle. There are a myriad of explanations for Bermuda Triangle; some are religious in nature, and claim it is believed that this Triangle is a way to hell. Others are based on mythology from the past and some even refer to extraterrestrials in one way or another. Several contain conspiracies or the secrets of the unexplored world.

So, we've only included the most widely-documented and well-known theories in this article. You'll be shocked by the number of theorists that exist all with their individual unique theory and each one more likely than the next.

Don't think this list as exhaustive. There are plenty of other options by yourself! It's not a bad thing... You might come up with an explanation of your own!

Chapter 2: What Is The Truth Lies?

With so many sources, both reliable and not making conclusions is an issue.

In the final analysis, it all boils down to which theory you're most comfortable with. Of course, there are theories and opinions but then there are factual and real.

Personally, I consider I am of the opinion that Bermuda Triangle mystery is not an unsolved mystery! Let me now clarify what I believe by this.

The Bermuda Triangle is a massive region that is awash with traffic. It is among the most frequently traveled sea routes across the globe. Its closeness the continent of America and the equator make it a popular air route too.

In the end, statistically speaking, if something is performed more than once the same thing will fail more often. If you are driving more than three times per month, the chance of it failing is very low. If you drive it more than three times per day, the chances of an accident increasing exponentially.

Let's return to the Triangle. It's a huge expanse of water, with hundreds of ships floating in it as well as planes flying over it. Therefore, it's only natural some of them are hit with unfortunate circumstances. Tragic? Sure, it's tragic! Is it a mystery that is baffling? It's not so.

Let's suppose that there are a thousand buses traveling between New York to Chicago every year. Ten of them crashes. It's a tiny fraction, isn't it? Imagine that 10000 buses travel between Beijing through Shanghai and one hundred of them crash. This is a total of one percent you think? What does 100 is more than ten suggest that the highway between Beijing to Shanghai will be cursed? It's not at all We can safely assume that if 10 000 buses were to travel across the country from New York to Chicago, 100 of them would be crashing on the highway also.

If you're me, this is what's happening within the Bermuda Triangle. Ask the marine insurers about the Bermuda Triangle. They are charged by risk. If the journey between points A and B is more hazardous in general and more dangerous than traveling from point C to D You can be certain that they'll charge higher for your first. Do they charge an additional charge on ships that pass in Bermuda Triangle? Bermuda Triangle? There's no way!

How was this "mystery" become a reality? I've got an idea for this!

The technological advances from the 1900s until the present has been enormous. Today, we live with standards that were previously inconceivable. It has brought many changes to our lives. one of them is scientific, critical thinking.

In the midst of this transformation in our thinking there are individuals on both ends in the range. We'll call them the believers and the superstitious.

As each decade passes increasing numbers of people are turning against religion and that places the believers in a tense situation. The moment Flight 19 made the headlines but there was a shoe on opposite foot. People who were skeptical couldn't understand what was going on. Of course, that's the issue with their stance rather than seeking to clarify what's going on it was better to explain that there was nothing going on!

If I were to make an educated guess, I'd suggest that Bermuda Triangle was created Bermuda Triangle became a mystery only because of that basic mistake. However it did give rise to an atmosphere of mystery and unpredictability that led to a whole new generation of modern day superstition.

Consider what might occur if this event was to occur in the present. I'd guess that it would be dismissed as a single event that has no significance statistically or any other explanation. Theories regarding the disappearance Malaysia Airlines Flight 370, for instance are based more on the possibility of foul play rather instead of supernatural reasons.

However, even though the time is over but it is not over. Bermuda Triangle mystery definitely had its moments, from its sly beginning to its climax when the public refused to take vessels or planes that went through the region until the flurry of rebuttals put the mystery to rest to rest in peace. The Bermuda Triangle will continue to be an interesting historical footnote as well as a mythological modern legend that is awaiting to be remade by the most creative artists in every medium.

The Bermuda Triangle should be viewed with admiration and fascination. It is possibly the very few of the kind, and a phenomenon that still has a sense of mystery in an time of ever-growing technology and knowledge.

Chapter 3: Similar Paranormal Phenomena
Around the World

"Similar" is defined as "similar" to mean "mysterious incident that took place a few of years ago, and has proved to be a worthy to be the subject of news coverage."

This is a top 7 list of similar paranormal phenomena all over the world! Bermuda Triangle Bermuda Triangle might be the most well-known, but believe me when I say there are many other "mysteries"!

Lake Anjikuni

In the month of November, 1930, in the frozen wilderness of northern Canada one trapper named Joe Labelle was looking for shelter to stay the night.

He was a familiar face to Inuit people, and in particular with Inuit people, particularly the Inuit villages of Anjikuni. The village's population at that time isn't known, but estimates vary from 25 to 2,000. So your estimation is as accurate as anyone else's!

Labelle went to the small village (or the town of a small size) in hopes of spending the night there, however, what he discovered was much colder than freezing blows that hit the rocks: The villagers had disappeared.

The scene was terrifying, and this might be an understatement. All of the items were intact: food, furs and rifles, kayaks, everything, as if it had been abandoned.

There are many inconsistencies within the tale of Labelle, but leaving the issue aside it's an interesting instance that shows what can happen when a tiny legend is blown out of significance. It's no surprise that this incident was made famous; however, the concept is equally terrifying and fascinating.

Modern-day Mounties ignore the tale as a urban legend and for many reasons. However, there are numerous versions that are floating around, and with such an overwhelming number of theories that range from (you probably guessed it) vampires to aliens that you'll have to look around and wonder was there really a real event in this case?

Bigelow Ranch

A UFO fan's top choice It is also referred to in the form of "the" Skinwalker Ranch and the Sherman Ranch.

The 480-acre (almost one area) property, which is located in northwest Utah is home to a multitude of strange sightings, animal rituals destructions, and a variety of bizarre incidents.

The mysterious events have been happening since the 1950s, nearly all the time, but one of the most terrifying stories about the ranch is related by Terry and Gwen Sherman, who bought the ranch in 1994.

The couple came across the large wolf roaming in the grass. It appeared calm, and they attempted to pet it. It was gentle enough to be with them, however it did end up grabbing an ox by its snout and paws through it's enclosure's bars.

Terry was able to shoot at the wolf using an assault rifle, but the bullets did not have any effect. Terry then tried shooting the wolf with a shotgun with the same results. The wolf escaped completely on its own, and the Shermans attempted to track it, however, its tracks were abruptly stopped and it appeared as if it had gone missing.

After the incident The couple was constantly confronted by frightening visions, including UFO sightings and intelligent floating orbs that burned their dogs, bizarre mysterious cryptids and horrific cattle brutalizations.

Bridgewater Triangle

The site offers a amount of the supernatural that everyone will enjoy, from UFOs and poltergeists all the way to the cryptids, and even the satanic religions.

The region is situated in the southeastern region of Massachusetts close to the southwest of Boston. It encompasses around 200 sq miles.

The reports began in the 70s. they describe tall hairy, ape-like beasts (think Bigfoot), massive bird-like pterodactyls with wingspan of around fifteen feet (thunderbirds) and occasionally the gargantuan blood-stained canine.

Certain reports mention the mutilation of animals, most often calves and cows, which are frequently attributed to Satanic religious cults.

In the case of UFO sightings, we can find all kinds of flying saucers, from massive orbs of flame. Apart from these usual UFO sightings there are many other objects have been observed like the mysterious helicopters that appear to be black.

Bennington Triangle

It's not just a coincidence that there's something strange happening in these Triangles!

The area of the triangle isn't well identified, but the middle of it is situated in the

Vermont's Glastenbury Mountain. It also covers some of the cities that include Bennington (hence its designation), Woodford, Shaftsbury and Somerset.

The reason for this triangle to be listed on this page is because of several people who mysteriously disappeared from the area between 1920 between 1920 and 1950. The tragic events were reported in two books written by Joseph A. Citro. in his book Shadow Child, Citro devoted several chapters to discussing the disappearances which occurred within the Bennington Triangle, citing several stories from the local folklore.

The most intriguing, if not frightening cases involved Paula Welden and James Tetford. Paula was an 18-year old college student Bennington College, went out to hike on the 1st December of 1946, but never returned. It was a tragedy enough, but one unanswered disappearance didn't create a mystery. But then James disappeared just three years afterward.

Today, the Bennington Triangle has been relegated to the background of the mystery fiction genre. The last person that disappeared in the region was Frieda Langer on the 28th of October in 1968.

It was only sixteen days following the time Paul Jephson had vanished. Frieda's body was not found after two weeks of intensive search efforts, which included aircrafts as well as around 300 people who were on the ground. Her body was finally discovered in May of next year, however the reason for her death could not be established. In all the disappearances that occurred in the Triangle Frieda's body was the only one to be recovered.

It's quite odd, doesn't you think? The disappearances ceased when the body was discovered.

The Mothman

Have you heard of Point Pleasant, West Virginia? It's a little odd in this particular context does it not? Point Pleasant's name Point Pleasant was previously quite appropriate, however, it's since been encased in mysterious, dark instances.

Why? The Mothman!

The frightful humanoid monster has terrorized Point Pleasant from 1966 to 1967. In all, there were more than 100 reports from various residents. But the elusive cryptid/monster/mutant/boogeyman didn't stop there! It's since been seen in various locations like Cornwall, England; Chihuahua, Mexico; Pripyat, Ukraine as well as Santiago de Chile, Chile.

It is believed that the Mothman frequently appears as a warning of misfortune which makes his appearance far more terrifying due to the message they carry than the meaning of his appearance.

The Mothman's presence seemed so amazing to the residents from Point Pleasant that they erected an honorary statue of him, or perhaps to express gratitude when the mothman finally quit. It is a representation of his tall frame as well as his broad chest and wings.

San Luis Valley

Another dark and eerie location It's there's not another Triangle!

San Luis Valley, located in the southern part of Colorado is famous for its numerous UFO sightings, and even more alarmingly hundreds of animal mutilations.

Numerous people have witnessed UFOs within the region, sometimes at the same time, and if this doesn't shake you then the grotesque stories of animal mutilations will.

The grisly mutilations started in 1967 in the year that a horse by Snippy was found brainless. Snippy was discovered brainless having its neck bone totally cleaned. In the aftermath of Snippy's death hundreds upon hundreds of horrendous animal mutilations been reported across the region.

The shared traits include a complete absence of blood, and precisely-cut surgical cuts. Nothing that any predator of normal size could do. The most alarming thing is the fact that The majority of these incidents occur over night, in well-fed animals that had been otherwise in good health and healthy.

Many farmers have seen unusual light sources in the sky before they discovered the carcasses and have been led to believe that aliens may be involved. However, I am skeptical because I don't believe that super-advanced, secretive aliens could travel all up to Earth in order to mutilate farm animals.

But, no one seems to come up with a more plausible explanation; an investigation into the events hasn't been successful. If you're located in southern Colorado be sure to ensure your pet is in a tight-leash!

Baciu Forest

Locals describe this region as"the "Romanian Bermuda Triangle", and I'll try to give you a guess at where it is!

The mysterious forest is located in the midst of Transylvania and the majority of the inhabitants are scared of it. There is a belief that those who visit the forest experience numerous bizarre and frightening experiences (akin to the outside poltergeist). They are usually associated with strange and bizarre appearances and visions: UFOs strange immaterial structures that appear to be extraneous as well as sometimes, even physical structures.

A documentary on the forest's history reveals that the Transylvanian forests are rich in various paranormal or occult phenomena. Geometric spheres and other bright shapes are visible both all night long however, what is more frightening are the glimpses of humanoid animals as well as the dematerialization and materialization of bizarre nebula shapes.

Maybe the whole thing is an untruth that is propagated by the Transylvanian Chamber of Commerce, after all, these stories do draw in tourists. But I'm sure I'm not feeling as though I'm proving that!

Chapter 4: Theories, And Natural Explanations

The most popular and recent theory for solving mysteries surrounding the Bermuda Triangle is the hypothesis that methane hydrates may be the reason in order to explain the disappearances of planes and ships. Some of the most deep trenches on earth are located in this region. Any object that gets buried in them will likely never be found. Scientists speculate that there are massive deep ocean craters in the sea surface of Bermuda Triangle, resulting from methane gas leaks and oil trapped in different layers below the seafloor and is trapped in the form of methane hydrates.

There are lab experiments studies conducted in Australia which have shown that methane bubbles could cause a ship to sink due to their decreasing density of the sea. This is why methane explosions, which occur periodically within the Triangle do not provide enough buoyancy to ships, resulting in rapid sinking, without warning. Gas release is also cause of explosions and can also saturate the atmosphere with methane gas, leading to the airliners to sink.

The skeptical critics of this theory claim that there are huge reserves of methane-rich hydrates around the world as well as in areas that have no mysterious disappearances such as those of the Bermuda Triangle are reported. According to the U.S. Geological Survey proclaims that no significant releases of gas hydrates is thought to have occurred in the area of the Triangle for more than 15,000 years.

A popular and frequently popular theories for explanations is electromagnetic anomalies that occur throughout the Bermuda Triangle, that could cause fatal accidents due to the fact that navigators couldn't decide on the right direction to take. Captains of ships and pilots have reported issues with malfunctioning compasses, electronic gauges fuel gauges and voltage gauges. The area that is part of the Triangle is among the two areas on earth that magnetic compasses point towards the true north, which is known as compass variation. Navigators must compensate for this variance or else their vessel will be diverted. Another area of compass deviation is on the Pacific ocean known as"the "Devil's Sea." Some skeptical of the claim believe that the earth's magnetic field is constantly changing, there will always be compass changes and that there's no puzzle to be solved within this area of the Bermuda Triangle.

The geographic location of the Bermuda Triangle can be explained by the idea for the Gulf Stream, eradicating any evidence or evidence of missing vessels or planes. The ocean current is a part of the Gulf of Mexico, passing through the Straits of Florida and then into the North Atlantic, and then through the Bermuda Triangle area. If there's a crash of a plane or ship that is crashing into the sea the debris will flounder for until several hours later depending on the severity of the damage. In this time the wreckage will be quickly carried away along the Gulf Stream, until sinking beneath the stream, and eventually down to the seafloor. So, a catastrophe could start at one location and the remains could be transported to a different location of landing. The debris is quickly removed to ensure that the missing of a plane or ship is most likely to not be found.

Then there's the plausible idea of electronic fog according to Bruce Gernon, who was the only person who seen this phenomena completely, however, others have reported seeing a small portion of it. Gernon claims that he was able to lose 28 minutes of his time in the fog. The plane was missing from the radar until it was seen in Miami afterward. This fog acts as a portal or gateway to travel across time. Aircrafts and ships can be caught up in this fog of electronic activity, and in the end, all electronic devices starts to fail and eventually disappear, leaving no trace. It is believed the late John Hutchison, a physicist who experimented, developed this fog, calling the phenomenon "The Hutchison Effect."

Another theory that has been proven is that of an energy vortex, massive swirling vortex formations that suddenly pop up and disappear. The theory suggests that some vessels may have disappeared because of this phenomenon. Submerged pyramids, such as the crystal pyramids underwater found in the Bermuda Triangle have been observed to show vortexes that are occurring in the waters around them. These could be caused by a release of energy intrinsic to the area.

The theory behind the Sargasso Sea, details a unusual area that is located in the Bermuda Triangle. It is an attraction for boats that travel through the area. With extremely low winds, and a plethora of seaweed that is dense on the surface of the water The vessels are then motionless and are is surrounded by the ocean's currents all around. There are other theories that include pirates taking ships and explosive cargo that destroys the vessels. In this area, violent weather includes storms and rogue waves, as well as waterspouts hurricanes, as well as underwater earthquakes. There is a lot of seismic activity and variations have been seen in this region. The most popular theories suggest that UFOS and Aliens use vortexes, or wormholes or even The Lost City of Atlantis, to pass through the world via this area and the planes and ships who traverse these passageways. Human error is a prevalent idea, since even skilled navigators may make a mistake because the numerous islands of this region appear like one another and create confusion in the direction of the direction.

Chapter 5: Definition Of The Crystal Pyramids

The most astonishing discoveries of the Bermuda Triangle are the massive underwater Crystal Pyramids. These amazing pyramids are transparent structures that are made up of a kind of thick glass, which is a smooth crystal substance 300 meters in width and 200 meters high. Three times bigger in comparison to those of the Pyramid of Cheops in Egypt. They are located on top of the pyramids are two huge holes where the movement of seawater at a rate of high speed could result in surge waves as well as fog on the surface of the ocean. The crystal pyramids' properties serve as a natural electrical capacitor, by storing and collecting energy in them, and acting as energy amplifiers and energy accumulators.

A few members of Triangle researchers speculate that the structures could be linked to Atlantis, a city that was a major one of civilization. It is believed that the powerhouse of the island's pyramids were constructed of crystal, and had the tops being capped with crystallized substance. If Atlantis existed the pyramids could be remnants of a vortex machine that was believed to exist that was located on the ocean floor, or perhaps a warehouse for the inhabitants of Atlantis. Researchers have speculated that earthquakes might cause the pyramids to slide down to the floor of the ocean.

The Crystal Pyramids were originally discovered in the middle of the Bermuda Triangle, by Dr. Ray Brown of Mesa, Arizona, in the 1960's. The researcher had stumbled upon the structures while divers into the Bahamas. He conducted an investigation by swimming through an area of pyramids and gazing at the crystal clear sides, and not seeing growing anemones or seaweed. In the vicinity it was taken a mysterious crystal sphere to researchers for further research, which revealed fascinating characteristics associated with energy generation.

In 2012, American researchers, as well as French researchers who were conducting research in the Triangle found the underground pyramids rising out of the ocean. The findings were independently confirmed by diving teams of The U.S. And France. The researcher, Dr. Meyer Verlag with his German oceanographer team located the divers at an altitude of 2000m by using sonar. The results of his study were confiscated by the military, and further research are not permitted. The government and military have secured all data about the pyramids. Scientists continue to ask whether these pyramids contribute to the mysterious disappearances planes and boats within the Bermuda Triangle.

Bermuda Triangle: The Crystal Pyramids Under The Bermuda Triangle

Most Frequently Observed Disappearances in The Bermuda Triangle

Carroll A. Deering

On the 31st of January 1921 The Carroll A. Deering, an industrial schooner with five masted was on its way back from Maine after a trip to Rio de Janeiro of Brazil and then vanished. A team of investigators searched for the missing schooner. Some thought that the ship could have been running rum. The wreckage was discovered in Diamond Shoals, located off of Cape Hatteras in N.C. The vessel was found in good condition and abandoned, with the crew members missing.

Carroll A. Deering

C-54

On the 3rd of July 1947 the C-54 aircraft took off from Bermuda with six passengers on board and pilots who were experienced. The plane could be able of as many as 85 people. The plane was hit by a massive storm, but the issue is what caused the plane to go into the storm even though it could be prevented. In the beginning the plane was heading away from its intended course, and changing direction twice before heading straight towards the direction of the storm. There was an operator on the ground who received a weak SOS and then received an additional SOS but then a completely silence. The plane was never returned to sight.

C-54

Ellen Austin

In 1881, an oak schooner called Ellen Austin traveling on its route toward New York, saw a ship that was sailing with no crew aboard. She shifted some of her crew members to the ship to be able to pull it back to her. A storm squall cut off both ships' tracks and the second ship went missing. The ship is believed to have returned without anyone aboard however, it disappeared again without any trace. A variation on the tale is that, when the vessel came back, it was with another crew aboard and then it vanished again.

Ellen Austin

DC-3 Flight DC-3

On the 28th of December 1948, the plane Douglas Dakota DC-3 NC 16002 left at San Juan airport of Puerto Rico and headed towards Miami. It was a propeller powered aircraft that carried 28 passengers and three crew members. It was located in the area of 50 miles to the south of Florida within the Bermuda triangle with only 20 minutes left in the flight It vanished, and was never seen again.

DC-3 Flight DC-3

Flight 19

5 December 1945, a flight of training was conducted by TBM Avenger bombers of the US Navy known as Flight 19 was made up of 14 men who disappeared while flying across the Atlantic. The plan was to fly east from their Florida Naval base, for 120 miles and

then south for 73 miles returning 120 miles to return to their base for the completion of the training. The pilots did not return therefore the two Martin rescue Mariner aircrafts with a thirteen man crew were sent to find the men. A single of Mariners did not return and the plane was never located again. U.S. Navy investigators believe that the reason for disappearance may be due to a mishap in navigation, with the planes running out fuel. This is perhaps the most well-known incident in Bermuda Triangle. Bermuda Triangle, and one of the many aviation mysteries that are awe-inspiring.

Flight 19

Flight 441

On the 30th of October, 1954, a navy aircraft called Flight 441, took off with 42 passengers aboard. It was around 400 miles from the coastline at the time it disappeared completely. It vanished following regular communications was lost, and the plane disappeared from radar. The aircraft was fitted with enough flotation devices however, no evidence was discovered.

Flight 441

S.S. Marine Sulphur Queen

The 2nd of February, 1963 the 524-foot carrier carrying 15,000 tonnes of molten sulfur in heated tanks set sail out of Beaumont, Texas with 39 crew members, and headed for Norfolk, VA. The last message from the captain of the ship was a routine report on position broadcast on February 3 in 1963. The report indicated that the ship was close to Key West in the Florida Straits. The message was never received. Virginia After 3 days after which after 3 days, the Coast Guard found a single life jacket located 40 miles to the southwest of their previous location. Over the course of 19 days debris and life preservers were discovered, but not a crew or shipmen were discovered. The hypothesis for the disappearance is that the leak of sulphur could have led to an explosion or sulfur gas may be poisoning the crew members.

S.S. Marine Sulphur Queen

Mary Celeste

On the 4th December 1872 on the 4th of December, 1872, the Mary Celeste considered to be one of the ghost vessels of the Bermuda Triangle, was located at sea, stranded. All was fine, except for the crew members who were missing. The crew's belongings as well as the cargo were all still there. One of the theories suggested included food poisoning due to contaminated food items, or from weather-related events like sea earthquakes. The crew was never located.

Mary Celeste

USS Cyclops

On March 4, 1918 The Navy vessel, USS Cyclops, disappeared which resulted in the most tragic loss of lives to date in U.S. History. The ship vanished completely with 309 crew members when it left Barbados. of Barbados. The ship was carrying a complete load of manganese, which leads to the possibility that the vessel was loaded with more dense material. This may have caused the disappearance, since there was no evidence to support it.

USS Cyclops

Witchcraft

On the 22nd of December in 1967, a 23-foot cabin cruiser disappeared within the Bermuda Triangle region. Burrack, the owner Burrack was the one who had taken his boat off to look at the city lights in Miami with a companion. Around 9 p.m. Around 9 p.m., the Coast Guard states it received an inquiry from Burrack saying that his boat could be struck by something, however, the man did not seem to be concerned by the circumstances. They Coast Guard responded quickly in 19 minutes, however the boat and the two men were completely missing. It contained flotation devices, life jackets, and other life jackets but the two individuals and the ship never were found.

Witchcraft

Chapter 6: A Few Explanations Are Scientifically Based, Even Or At Least, In The Evidence

They include flatulence of the ocean (methane gas that releases from sediments of the ocean) as well as disruptions to the geomagnetic flux lines.

Environmental issues could be behind some, if certainly not all disappearances. Most Atlantic Hurricanes, tropical storms traverse Bermuda Triangle. Bermuda Triangle, and in the days before better weather forecasting the dangerous storms took the lives of numerous ships.

Additionally is there is the possibility that Gulf Stream can cause rapid change, often violent, in the weather. Furthermore, the huge number of islands within the Caribbean Sea creates many areas of shallow waters that could be hazardous to navigation by ship.

There is evidence that suggests there is evidence that the Bermuda Triangle is a place in which there is a "magnetic" compass can point toward "true" north in contrast to "magnetic" north.

1- 2 : 1 - U.S. Navy and U.S. Coast Guard claim that there aren't any supernatural explanations for catastrophes at sea.

Their experiences suggest that the natural forces and the human sabotaging exceed even the most bizarre science fiction. They say that there are there are no official maps available which define what constitutes Bermuda Triangle. Bermuda Triangle. According to the U. S. Board of Geographic Names does not recognize the Bermuda Triangle as an official name, and it does not have an official record of the region.

The ocean has always been a mystery area to us, and when poor weather or bad navigation is the case it can turn out to be very dangerous. This is the case all over the globe. It is not clear to suggest that mysterious disappearances are occurring with more number in Bermuda Triangle than in any other vast, well-traveled region within the sea.

3-4 : Myths and Mysteries of the Bermuda Triangle

The Bermuda Triangle is a region within the Atlantic Ocean running between Puerto Rico, Bermuda, and Miami has been linked to the disappearance and deaths of more than 8,000 people from the mid-19th century onward.

Fig . 1: Portrait of the legend Lost Squadron & plane "Flight 19" that was believed to have vanished to Bermuda Triangle shortly after WWII. It is part of the LIFE Picture Collection via Getty Images

* While the exact figure isn't available, at most 50 aircrafts and 20 ships have vanished in the Triangle and often without leaving a trail.

*The Bermuda Triangle has become the topic of myths, legends and conspiracy theories.

* Some have referred to it as The Devil's Triangle.

Other have referred the area by the name of Limbo of the Lost or the Hoodoo Sea. However, to the majority they are known as the Bermuda Triangle, a stretch of water located in the Atlantic Ocean known to swallow planes and ships.

For centuries, the Bermuda Triangle has been mystified as a terrifying stretch of ocean, in which pilots and sailors are likely to be disconnected from the nature and vanish for ever.

While the US government is not recognizing Bermuda Triangle as a real geographical area or threat, the Bermuda Triangle as an actual geographical location or threat however, the Bermuda Triangle's legends have created a picture of mystery, death and terror.

We'll break down the story of the Triangle and some of its most famous stories:

Bermuda and the vast stretch of sea that surrounds is, was subjected into legend for long periods of time. Some believe that Shakespeare's"The Tempest "The Tempest" is based on stories of pirates and sorcery in the area.

Fig . 3 Admiral Somers is able to land his ship, Bermuda, 1609 (c1880)

Admiral Sir Geirge Somers (1554-1610) was the pioneer of Bermuda, an English colonies of Bermuda and Bermuda stories about the shipwreck of his are believed to be the inspiration for Shakespeare's play "The Tempest'. The Print Collector/Getty Images.

As Christopher Columbus passed through the Bermuda Triangle on his first voyage to the world of the future and recorded the moment an explosion of fire was spotted on the sea and caused a mysterious light to be seen in the distance weeks afterward.

Fig . 1 - 4 : Christopher Columbus. Wikipedia

1 - In 1881, legend claims that Ellen Austin, a ship traveling across the Atlantic from Liverpool towards New York, encountered a "ghost ship" in the Bermuda Triangle and things quickly got out of hand.

The moment Ellen Austin Ellen Austin approached the foggy waters of the Sargasso Sea -- a region that is part of the Atlantic Ocean that overlaps with the Bermuda Triangle -- the crew was greeted by a fully stocked abandoned ship.

The idea was to take advantage of valuable cargo they sent a few of their men aboard to be occupying the vessel and travel for the rest of the voyage in tandem.

However, a severe storm swiftly caused the two ships to be separated, and when they reconnected the following day, there was no sign of any crew visible.

Fig . 1-5 : Illustration of a fog-shrouded ship at sea. Shutterstock The ship was more abandoned , but it was still filled with valuable materials, and Captain Ellen Austin tried boarding it again.

However, when the crew members stepped on board for the second time the thick and blinding fog came into the ship and separated them.

As the fog dissipated when the fog finally cleared, when the fog cleared, the "ghost" craft had totally disappeared, as per stories published in the current newspapers.

1-5: In 1895, Joshua Slocum, the first man to solo sail around the globe, vanished during a trip between Martha's Vineyard to South America

Slocum would have lost at sea He was known as an outstanding sailor and his disappearance in the middle of the night is now believed to be due to the Bermuda Triangle.

Fig . 1 - Poster advertising"sailing alone around the world "Sailing All Alone Around The World" from Lieutenant Joshua Slocum, 1903. Smith Collection/Gado/Getty Images

The year 1918 saw the United States Navy's most powerful and fastest fuel vessel was The USS Cyclops, disappeared en traveling to in the Caribbean towards Baltimore having 309 people on board. They left no evidence of what transpired.

Fig . 1-7: The USS Cyclops which disappeared in Bermuda after returning from a voyage to Brazil in March 1918. Apic/Getty Images 1-6 : Although well-equipped with emergency equipment as well as signaling however, the USS Cyclops gave no warning that something was going on at sea. The legendary vessel that once provided help during WWI and transported many tons of manganese ore was simply gone without any trace.

Theories of mutiny, storms torpedoes, and poison were being circulated However, none of them made any sense.

There was collision and the debris was found, where is it? What was the reason for no distress signal? What could have happened to it? taken when it did not have the fuel required to travel long distances?

In the meantime, people began to think about strange creatures like the gigantic squid, as well as the tangled web of Bermuda Triangle, as reported by The Washington Post. "There was any more mysterious mystery in the history of the Navy than the disappearance of the last month of the U.S.S. Cyclops." Navy Secretary Josephus Daniels wrote in 1919.

In 1941 in 1941, the Navy ship known as The USS Proteus was carrying 58 passengers as well as a load in ore to St. Thomas to the East Coast when it suddenly disappeared in the Bermuda Triangle. A month later the ship's sister, The USS Nereus, disappeared along with 61 passengers on similar routes.

Fig . 1-8: The USS Proteus. Stevens/Fairfax Media through Getty Images

After 1945, the myth of the Bermuda triangle took hold after five TBM Avenger torpedo bombers took off from a naval station in Ft. Lauderdale, Fl. and vanished into the Atlantic Ocean before completing their mission.

"Flight 19" was set to finish an exercise lasting three hours that involved flying east for bombing runs, after which it flew over Grand Bahama Island, and then pivoting to the toward the southwest to return to the home base.

Fig . 1-9 : The model for American Navy Avenger planes, torpedo-bombers , that vanished within the Bermuda Triangle Apic/Getty Images

However Captain Charles C. Taylor became anxious after his compass stopped working and he was convinced it was because the aircrafts appeared to be heading to the incorrect direction. He instructed his team to fly north -- believing he was headed towards Florida however, he was actually going further to the Atlantic.

1-7: As the planes approached closer to the Bermuda triangle the signals of their aircraft began to fade.

The report is from the History channel. In the end, all communications were shut down and the planes never ever again.

The last thing to be recorded in the emails of Flight 19 passengers were eerie reports about their location: "Everything looks strange, even the ocean," said one pilot.

Fig . 1-10 : A portrait of the the legend Lost Squadron & plane "Flight 19" that was believed to have vanished in the Bermuda Triangle shortly after WWII. It is part of the LIFE Picture Collection via Getty Images

Then he added: "It looks like we are in white water...we're totally lost."

It was reported that the disappearance of Flight 19 was so baffling that the official Navy report stated that it happened "as as if they'd travelled on to Mars."

In 1948 in 1948, the DC-3 commercial flight disappeared in the Triangle with 29 passengers and two crew members on their way towards Miami.

Fig . 1-11 : DC-3 aircraft, 1937. Underwood Archives/Getty Images 50 miles before arriving in the city, the pilot of the aircraft, Robert Lindquist, radioed the Miami Airport for landing instructions.

The radio signal was silenced and the plane never returned. In the same year the British Avro Tudor aircraft, dubbed "Star Tiger" disappeared from the Bermuda Triangle without a trace.

1-8: Twenty-five passengers and 6 crew were aboard No debris or other information was ever discovered.

As per BBC News, the official report concluded that "What occurred in this particular investigation will never be revealed so the destiny of Star Tiger will remain unsolved."

Fig . 1-12 : 1948, British Avro Tudor Plane. Popperfoto/Getty Images 1-9 : One year later on the 29th of October 1949, a G-AGRE aircraft named "Star Ariel" left in Bermuda for Kingston, Jamaica

The flight then lost communication after switching to Kingston frequency, which is above that of the Bermuda triangle. While the weather was clean and the flight seemed to be in good shape but it wasn't heard or seen again.

Fig . 1-13: Kingston Jamaica city port at sunrise. Valery Sharifulin Getty Images

In 1963 in 1963, it was reported that the SS Marine Sulphur Queen, an enormous tanker vessel carrying 39 passengers as well as sulfur molten was last seen off the coast of southern Florida. After two weeks of searching the rescue crew only found a few fragments of wreckage and life-saving devices.

Fig . 1-14 : Two life-saving devices and a foghorn bearing the title "S.S. Marine Sulphur Queen" written on them are scrutinized by Coast Guardsmen in this. Getty Images

The expression "Bermuda Triangle" was first created by Vincent Gaddis in a 1964 pulp magazine article entitled "The Deathly Bermuda Triangle."

Fig . 1-15 : The triangle that is in the question. NOAA

In his tale, Gaddis outlined several mysteries of the Triangle which bolstered the notion that this area of the ocean is a dangerous zone.In 1967, people on the 590-foot cargo vessel Sylvia L. Ossa became victims of the Triangle's mysteries after the ship mysteriously disappeared, with only 37 aboard. Although debris, including a life-saving device and a lifeboat was discovered but the vessel was never found again.

Fig . 1-16: The Coast Guard is still searching for the Panamanian cargo ship "Sylvia L. Ossa" in the notorious Bermuda Triangle where it was reported to have a mission with 37 crew members. AP Photo

In 1978, a skilled pilot named Irving Rivers departed from the US Virgin Islands on a solo flight to collect passengers from St. Thomas. The weather was pleasant and Rivers was just a mile away from the point of landing when his lights disappear from radar. Search teams were assigned to search for him, however, the plane was not discovered.

Fig . 1-17: View of St. Thomas Island, where passengers waited for a flight which would never arrive. Getty Images

In 1984 it was reported that the Cessna plane that was departing from Fort Lauderdale, and en journey towards an island located in the Bahamas was completely wiped out of radar signals before sinking to the sea. There was no radio signals sent or received, and even though one person claimed to have witnessed the plane fall into the sea but no remains were discovered.

Fig . 1-18 : 1984 Cessna plane.Victor Colin Sumner/Fairfax Media Getty Images

Theories regarding The Bermuda Triangle have been rampant for a long time. Some believe the Triangle's mysteries may be due to an alien presence. Others believe it's the mighty operations from the underwater kingdom of myth. Atlantis.

Fig . 1-19: 3D illustration inspired by the myth of the city that was lost to Atlantis and the underwater city rendering Fer Gregory/Shutterstock 1-10: Bermuda Triangle stories have been proved to be more fiction than reality

It is important to note that the US government has never acknowledged the area of ocean as a potentially dangerous place, and there's no evidence that suggests disappearances are occurring with any greater frequency in the Triangle than other large areas of ocean.

Fig . 1-20 : Aerial view of Bermuda. Island of Bermuda. Getty Images Scientists have attributed the numerous disappearances to fast and severe weather shifts as well as shallow water levels and methane gas explosions that occur in the sea.

Fig . 1-21 : The churning of the hurricane in the waters close to the Bermuda Triangle. NOAA through Getty Images

In January of 2020 the remains of SS Cotopaxi was found off the coast of Florida. Many believed that the ship had disappeared in 1925 due to some enigmatic reasons connected with Bermuda Triangle. Bermuda Triangle. The discovery of the ship finally ended the speculations.

Fig. 1-22: Researchers diving to find out more about the remains of the SS Cotopaxi, which disappeared around century ago. Science Channel

Scientists might have achieved a major breakthrough in figuring out the mystery surrounding Bermuda Triangle. Bermuda Triangle.

The reason why giant squids that once sounded like a kraken of deep waters, remain puzzled scientists more than 150 years after their discovery.

The Bermuda Triangle, also known as the Devil's Triangle, is a vaguely defined region in the western region of the North Atlantic Ocean where a large number of ships and aircraft are believed to have vanished in mysterious circumstances. Most reliable sources deny the notion that there's any mystery.123

Fig. 1-23 : One variant of the Bermuda Triangle area 1-10-1 : Origins

The first hint of strange disappearances from the Bermuda area was reported in the 17th of September 1950, article that was published by The Miami Herald (Associated Press) by Edward Van Winkle Jones.4Two years after, Fate magazine published "Sea Mystery at Our Back Door",56a short piece written from George Sand covering the loss of several vessels and planes as well as the destruction from Flight 19, a group of five US Navy Grumman TBM Avenger torpedo bombers in the course of a training mission. Sand's article was the very first to describe the now-known triangular space in which the loss occurred as well as being the first to propose that there was a supernatural component in this particular Flight 19 incident.

1-10-2: Flight 19 alone would be discussed again in the April edition of American Legion magazine

7 In the book, author Allan W. Eckert wrote that the pilot was heard saying "We are in white water. Nothing seems to be quite right. We're not sure where we are. The water is green, not white." He also stated that officials from the Navy board of inquiry said they believed that planes "flew off towards Mars. "8

On February 14, 1964 Vincent Gaddis wrote an article titled "The Deadly Bermuda Triangle" in the pulp magazine Argosy in which he claimed that Flight 19 and other disappearances were part of a series of bizarre events that occurred in the region.9The following one year Gaddis extended the article to a book, Invisible Horizons.10

Others have elaborated on Gaddis his ideas, including: John Wallace Spencer (Limbo of the Lost, 1969; repr. 1973);11Charles Berlitz (The Bermuda Triangle, 1974);12Richard Winer (The Devil's Triangle, 1974),13and many others who all remained true to the same supernatural elements as outlined by Eckert.14

1-11: Triangle Area

The Gaddis Argosy piece defined areas of the triangle, 9 naming its vertex locations being Miami; San Juan, Puerto Rico; and Bermuda. The subsequent writers did not always adhere to this definition.15Some writers provided distinct boundaries and vertices for the triangle in total, with the size varied from 1,300,000 to 3,900,000. km2(500,000 to 1,510,000 sq mi).15"Indeed there were writers who extend it as far as even the Irish coast. "2Consequently the decision of what kind of accidents took place within the triangle will depend on the writer wrote about them.15

1-12 : Criticism of Concept

1-12-1 : Larry Kusche

Larry Kusche, author of The Bermuda Triangle Mystery: Solved (1975)1argued that many of the assertions of Gaddis and his successors were exaggerated, doubtful or unproven. Kusche's study revealed a myriad of inconsistencies and errors between Berlitz's narratives and the statements from participants, eyewitnesses and other people involved in the first incidents. Kusche pointed out instances in which relevant details were not reported like the disappearance of yachtsman from around the world Donald Crowhurst, which Berlitz claimed to be an unsolved case, despite overwhelming evidence against it. Another instance was the ore-carrier that was described by Berlitz as missing without trace three days after leaving an Atlantic port, when it was lost for three days from the same port as the name, within the Pacific Ocean. Kusche claimed that a significant portion of the events that led to speculation about the Triangle's mysterious influence actually occurred outside the boundaries of. The majority of his research was straightforward to look through papers from the period prior to the date of incidents that were reported, and then find stories about events that might be relevant, like weather anomalies, which were not mentioned in disappearance reports.

Kusche said: The number of aircraft and ships reported missing in this region was not significantly higher relative to elsewhere in the ocean.

In a region that is frequently hit by tropical cyclones instances of disappearances which did occur were generally not disproportionate, unprobable or mysterious.

In addition, Berlitz and other writers are often oblivious to these storms, or even depict disappearances that occurred under calm conditions, when meteorological evidence clearly disproves this.

The figures themselves were exaggerated due to a lack of research. The disappearance of a boat, for instance, would have been not reported, however its eventual (if late) arrival back at port could not be.

A few disappearances have actually not occurred. A plane crash was reported to have occurred in 1937 off Daytona Beach, Florida, before hundreds of witnesses. A review of local newspapers found nothing.

The myth that surrounds Bermuda Triangle Bermuda Triangle is a manufactured mystery perpetuated by authors who, either intentionally or not, employed falsehoods, incorrect reasoning and sensationalism.1

In a study from 2013 that was released in 2013, The World Wide Fund for Nature identified the 10 most hazardous waters for shipping However, Bermuda Triangle was not one of them. Bermuda Triangle was not among them.1617 1-12-2: Further Responses

The UK Channel 4 television program The Bermuda Triangle (1992)18was being produced by John Simmons of Geofilms for the Equinox series The market for marine insurance Lloyd's of London was asked to determine if an unusually high amount of vessels had been sunk inside the Bermuda Triangle area. Lloyd's found that a large number of vessels had not been sunk there.3Lloyd's does not charge more rates for traveling through this region. United States Coast Guardrecords confirm their findings. Actually, the amount of disappearances that are believed to have occurred is comparatively insignificant when compared to the amount of aircrafts and ships that travel through the area regularly on a daily basis.1

1-13: The Coast Guard is also officially skeptical of the Triangle

In addition, they gather and make available, through their research, a lot of evidence in opposition to many of the stories reported by Triangle authors.

In one of these incidents, which involved the 1972 explosion and sinking of tanker V. A. Fogg The Coast Guard photographed the wreck and found several bodies.19This contrasts with the Triangle author's assertion that all the bodies were gone and were only missing the captain, who was discovered sitting at his desk and clutching an empty coffee cup.11

Furthermore, V. A. Fogg was sunk in the Gulf of Texas but not near the boundaries that are commonly accepted for the Triangle.

The Nova/Horizon episode The Case of the Bermuda Triangle that aired on the 27th, 1976. It was highly critical, declaring that "When we go back to the source or to the people who were who were involved in the Triangle, all mystery vanishes. Science is not required to answer any questions regarding the Triangle since those questions aren't relevant in the first place ... Planes and ships behave in the Triangle exactly the same way as they do everywhere else. "2

1-13-1 : Skeptical researchers such as Ernest Taves[20] or Barry Singer[21] have noticed that the paranormal and mysteries are extremely popular and lucrative

This has led to the creation of huge amounts of material about topics like and the Bermuda Triangle. They were able show that certain pro-paranormal materials are often false or incorrect, yet the producers continue to promote it. They have also stated they are biased favor of television specials and other media that are supportive of that Triangle investigation, but in opposition to thoroughly researched material when it promotes an skeptic's view.

Benjamin Radford, an author and researcher in the field of scientific paranormal investigations in an interview regarding the Bermuda Triangle that it could be difficult to locate an aircraft that went missing in the sea because of the large search area and even though the disappearance could be a mystery, that does not make it supernatural or unsolvable. Radford added the necessity of double-checking the information, as the mystery of this mystery Bermuda Triangle had been created by those who were unable to check so.22

1-14. Hypothetical explanation Strategies

People who accept this Bermuda Triangle as a real phenomenon have suggested a variety of explanations.

1-15: Paranormal Explanations

Triangle writers have utilized various supernatural theories to explain the happenings. One theory places the blame on technology that was left over from the mythical continent called Atlantis. The most frequently cited connection to the Atlantis mythology can be the submerged rock structure referred to as the Bimini Road on the Island of Bimini located in the Bahamas located situated in the Triangle according to some definitions. The followers of the alleged psychic Edgar Cayce take his prediction that evidence of Atlantis could be discovered in 1968 as refers towards the discovery of Bimini Road. Some believe that the structure is the result of a wall, road or some other construction, but Bimini Road is believed to be a natural structure. Bimini Road is of natural origin.23Other authors claim that the events were caused by UFOs.2425Charles

Berlitz, who wrote numerous books on strange phenomena, has a list of theories that attribute the loss of the Triangle to mysterious or unproven forces.12

1-16: Natural Explanations

Compass problems are among the frequently used phrases in Triangle incidents. Although some have suggested that strange magnetic anomalies local to the area might be found in the region,26 such anomalies have not been observed.

Compasses are able to detect magnetic changes with respect to magnetic poles, an observation that navigators have been aware of for decades. The magnetic (compass) north, and geographical (true) north can be the same except for a few locations, for instance at the time of 2000 within the United States, only those locations that lie along a line across Wisconsin through the Gulf of Mexico.27But the general public might not be aware and may believe that there's something awe-inspiring about an compasses "changing" throughout an area as big as the Triangle as it will.1

Fig . 1-24 : False-color picture of Gulf Stream flowing north through the western Atlantic Ocean. (NASA)

1-17: Gulf Stream

It is believed that the Gulf Stream is a major surface current that is primarily driven by thermohaline circulation . It begins in the Gulf of Mexico and then flows through the Straits of Florida into the North Atlantic. It is an ocean within a river as well as, just like the ocean, it could and transport floating objects. Its maximum speed of 2 meters per second (6.6 ft/s).28A tiny plane that is making an attempt to land on water or a boat with engine issues could be swept away from its position because of the force.

1-18 : Human Error

A common and frequently frequently cited reasons in official inquiries pertaining in the case of the destruction of an aircraft or vessel is that of human error.29Human determination may have led the businessman Harvey Conover to lose his sailing vessel, Revonoc, as he was sailing into an incoming storm to the to the south from Florida on January 1st 1958.30

1-19: Violent Weather

The powerful hurricanes occur in tropical waters. They have in the past cost many lives as well as caused trillions of damages. In

1502, the sinking of Francisco de Bobradilla's Spanish ship in 1502 was very first documented instance of a devastating storm. These storms have in past led to a variety of incidents that are related with the Triangle. A lot of Atlantic hurricanes traverse the Triangle as they make their way back to into the Eastern Seaboard, and, prior to the advent of the weather satellites, ships usually were not aware of the approaching storm.

Fig . 1-25: Tracks of all Atlantic hurricanes from 1851 to 2019. Many storms travel through in the Bermuda Triangle.

1-19-1 : A massive cold downdraft was thought to be the reason for the sinking of Pride of Baltimore on May 14, 1986.

A crew member of the sunken ship observed the wind suddenly changed direction and increased its speed between 32km/h (20 miles per hour) up to between 97 and 145 kilometers per hour (60-90 miles per hour). The National Hurricane Center satellite specialist, James Lushine, stated "during extremely unstable weather conditions the upswing of cold air out of the sky can strike the ground like a bomb, and explode outwards like a massive storm of water and wind. "31

Similar incidents occurred in Concordia in 2010, which was off on the shores of Brazil. Scientists are currently examining the possibility that "hexagonal" clouds might be the cause of these 170-mph (270 kilometers/hour) "air bombs".32

1-20: Methane Hydrates

A possible explanation for disappearances is based on the existence of vast methane-hydrate fields (a kind that is natural gas) in the continental shelves.33

Research conducted in Australia have demonstrated that bubbles could, in fact sink a model vessel by reducing in the volume of water. Any debris that rises to the surface will quickly disperse any debris that rises to the surface would be quickly dispersed by any wreckage that comes to the surface will be rapidly dispersed by the Gulf Stream. It is believed the possibility that methane explosions on a regular basis (sometimes known as "mud volcanic eruptions") can result in areas of frothy waters which are not suitable for providing sufficient buoyancy to ships. If this is the case, this region that forms around a ship might cause it to sink quickly in a matter of minutes without notice.

Fig . 1-26: Worldwide distribution of verified or inferred offshore gas-hydrate bearing sediments in 1996.

Publications of the USGS contain large quantities of undersea hydrates from all over the world which includes Blake Ridge, which is located in the Blake Ridge area, off the coast of the southeast United

States.37However according to the USGS the USGS, there are no significant gas hydrate releases are thought to have occurred in the Bermuda Triangle for the past 15,000 years.3

1-21 : Notable Incidents

1-21-1: HMS Atalanta (1844)

The sail-training ship HMS Atalanta (originally called HMS Juno) was lost along with her entire crew shortly after setting out on Royal Naval Dockyard, Bermuda in search of Falmouth,

England on the 31st of January 1880.38It was thought that she was sunk during a storm that traversed her path shortly after she left in the first place, and that her crew , which was composed mostly of trainees with no experience could have contributed to the. The hunt for the cause of her death received worldwide attention in the period (connection is often drawn to the 1878 sinking of the training vessel HMS Eurydice, which foundered when it left at the Royal Naval Dockyard in Bermuda to Portsmouth on March 6) The ship was believed to have been the victims of the mysterious triangle a claim which was completely refuted in the research by author David Francis Raine in 1997.3940414243

Fig . 1-27: HMS Atalanta

11-2 : USS Cyclops (AC-4)

The event that resulted in the largest loss of lives during the entire history of the US Navy not related to combat took place in the case of collier Cyclops with a complete amount of manganese having one engine not in action, disappeared without trace with 309 crew members following March 4th, 1918, shortly after leaving from the Caribbean island Barbados. While there isn't much basis for any one theory, several theories exist, with some blaming storms, while others suggest capsizing and others suggesting conflict-related enemy activity was the primary factor at fault for the loss.4445In In addition Two of Cyclops's twin ship, Proteus and Nereus were later lost in the North Atlantic during World War II. Both vessels were carrying huge quantities of metallic ore, similar to the one that was loaded onto Cyclops on her final journey. In all three instances, structural failure caused by overloading more dense cargo than was originally intended is thought to be as the primary cause for sinking.

11-21-3 Carroll. Deering

Carroll A. Deering, the five-masted schooner that was constructed during 1919 was discovered abandoned and hard aground at Diamond Shoals, near Cape Hatteras, North Carolina, on the 31st of January 1921. FBI investigations into Deering examined, and but did not rule out, several theories about why and how the vessel was abandoned, such as pirates and domestic Communist destruction and the involvement of rum-runners.46

Fig . 1-28: Schooner Carroll A. Deering, as seen from the Cape Lookout lightvessel on January 29, 1921, just two days before she was discovered abandoned at sea in North Carolina. (US Coast Guard)

1-1-4 19.

Flight 19 was a training flight with five TBM Avenger torpedo bombers that went missing on the 5th of December 1945, as they flew in the Atlantic. The plan of flight for the squadron was to fly them due east of Fort Lauderdale for 141 mi (227 km) and then north for 73 miles (117 km) and back to Fort Lauderdale for a final 140-mile (230-kilometre) section to finish the mission. The plane did not return to Fort Lauderdale. The disappearance was blamed to Navy investigators to a navigational error which led to the aircraft not having enough fuel.

One of the search and rescue planes that was deployed to search for them one of the aircrafts, an PBM Mariner with a 13-man crew, was also missing. A tanker on Florida's coast reported seeing an explosion Florida was reported to have witnessed an explosion47 and seeing a large oil slick as it searched for survivors. The weather had turned turbulent by the time that incident.48According to sources from the time, the Mariner was a victim of explosions caused by leaks of vapour when it was loaded with fuel and fuel, which could be for a long search and rescue mission.

1-21-5: Star Tiger and Star Ariel

G-AHNP Star Tiger vanished in January, 1948 during flight from Azores to Bermuda G-AGRE Star Ariel went missing on the 17th of January, 1949, during a flight between Bermuda in the Azores to Kingston, Jamaica. The two aircrafts were Avro Tudor IV passengers aircrafts owned by British South America Airways.49

Both aircrafts were operating at the limits of their capabilities and even the slightest glitch or flaw within the aircraft could prevent these planes from reaching tiny island.1

1-1-6 1948 Airborne Transport DC-3 (DST) Disappearance

On the 28th of December 1948 the Douglas DC-3 aircraft, number NC16002, vanished while flying that was taking off from San Juan, Puerto Rico in the Caribbean to Miami. The aircraft was never found or the passengers aboard, was discovered. The Civil Aeronautics Board investigation found that there was not enough information for determining the what might be the reason for the disappearance.50

1-21-7 : Connemara IV

A pleasure boat was discovered floating on Bermuda's Atlantic South of Bermuda on the 26th of September 1955. It's usually mentioned in the tales (Berlitz, Winer)1213that the crew disappeared while the boat survived being in the sea for three hurricanes. It was 1955. Atlantic hurricane season records the hurricane Ione being close by between the 14th and 18th of September The hurricane season began on September

14, with Bermuda being hit by wind gusts of almost gale force.1In his second book about Bermuda Triangle, Winer wrote: Bermuda Triangle, Winer quoted from a letter he received from Mr. J.E. Challenor from Barbados: 51

In the early morning of September 22, Connemara IV lay to an untidy mooring within the openroadstead in Carlisle Bay. Due to the imminent storm, the owner re-torched the mooring ropes , and set two anchors on the water. There was nothing else he could do because the exposed mooring was the only anchorage he had. ... Then, in Carlisle Bay, the sea following the impact ofHurricane Janet was breathtaking and a danger. Connemara IV's owner Connemara IV was able to observe that she was gone. An investigation showed that she had pulled her moorings, and then gone out to the sea.

Chapter 7: The History And Mystery Of The Bermuda Triangle

Bermuda Triangle Bermuda Triangle is a triangular part of the Atlantic Ocean between Bermuda, San Juan, and Miami. The Bermuda Triangle has also been the location of disappearances of vessels and planes as well as sightings of ghost ships as well as weather anomalies. The first record that we have of the region's strange events originates by Christopher Columbus, who claimed to have witnessed a burst flame erupting from the ocean and also a mysterious illumination that took place within a couple of weeks

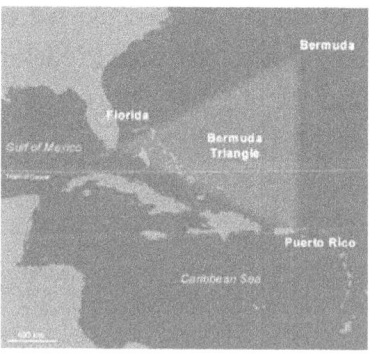

Fig . 2 : Bermuda Triangle

1-1) 1. One of the first events in the Triangle that we know of in numerous details is the so-called "ghost ship" that was discovered in 1881.

In the hazy weather of the Triangle the crew of Ellen Austin's spot an abandoned ship. It was in good shape, well-maintained, and carried many things in the. The crew, convinced they've have hit the jackpot, invites some crew members to help sail the ship towards their goal. A storm ripped apart the two of vessels. When they returned to the Ellen Austin found the ship and re-discovered it the ship was abandoned. the crew they sent missing, but again, the ship was safe and the cargo in the vessel. It is the Ellen Austin, against all rationality and common sense decides to go back and sends crew members to take the vessel alongside. They lose each other in the thick fog. It was the Ellen Austin made it to her destination, but she never seen the other vessel or the crew they lost.

2 : Ellen Austin was not the only ship that experienced bizarre experience in the Triangle in addition,"the "ghost vessel" did not have to be the only ship to disappear.

It was in 1895 that Joshua Slocum, the first person to solo sail around the globe, disappeared probably in this area. In 1918 the USS Cyclops, as well as her crew of more than

300 people vanished without trace. The time was 1918 and the president Woodrow Wilson said:

"Only God and the sea can tell what was happening to the great ship."

This was followed by the disappearance in 1941 of USS Proteus and her crew

This was followed by the loss in the spring of 1941 for the USS Proteus and her crew of one person on that same road.

Ships weren't all the afflicted vehicles in the Triangle. In 1945, five Avengerclass torpedo bombers vanished in the region after departing in the direction of Fort Lauderdale.

At this point, the supposed radio transmissions were: "Everything looks strange, even the ocean." and "It seems like we're in the white waters... it appears that we are totally lost." Prior to radio contact, the information was lost. The official Navy report said it was "as as if they'd travelled to Mars."

3: Between 1948 and 1949 3 : In 1948-1949, at Least Three planes disappeared

A DC-3 commercial aircraft with 31 passengers disappeared in the Triangle as it headed to Miami. The captain called Miami for instructions on landing but was not received with silence, and the plane never

ever seen again. Star Tiger disappeared in the same year. Star Tiger disappeared the same year, along with 31 passengers. It was reported that the Star Ariel disappeared from Bermuda to Kingston with clear skies. It also lost contact with radio. The year 1963 saw a tanker vessel that carried 39 people disappeared, leaving only a handful of wreckage and life-saving devices to help determine the fate of the ship.

4 - 5 4: The Mystery

Today, bizarre disappearances and strange events have been reported from Bermuda Triangle. Bermuda Triangle. Compasses, it is said, do not function. Signals from radios are not received.

It also works in a variety of magical ways, where we can see the experiences of those who lost radio contact , and then having been seen for the final time. Really, how can we be sure that the DC-3 flight was not heard from as they radioed Miami and never heard again, with no proof or remains of survivors left to follow.

Fig . 2 The USS Cyclops during 1911.

"The Black Pearl? I've heard of tales. She's been hunting ships and towns for nearly 10 years. There aren't any survivors left.

No survivors? What is the source of the stories? originate, I'm wondering?"

-an exchange between prisoners and Capt. Jack Sparrow in DIsney's Pirates of the Carribean film

While we can laugh, certain stories were exaggerated, and then elaborated throughout the years to make more credible reports as well as create the Triangle ever more mysterious. However, the stories must originate from somewhere. What's the root of all the turmoil that has occurred in the Bermuda Triangle?

2-5: Theories

2-5-1: SUPERNATURAL

The year 1974 was the time that Charles Berlitz (yes, of the Berlitz fame for his language-learning) suggested in 1974 that the Triangle was in some way connected to the city that was once Atlantis. Others have also pondered this idea, even going as far to suggest that Atlantis is located in the middle of the ocean and utilizes its "crystal energy" to destroy planes and ships. The motivations behind the phenomenon aren't fully understood.

Others have suggested that something other than the ocean is responsible for the disappearances and failures : an alien base underwater. It is possible that they aren't like aliens in Signs which are damaged by water. Some have said that alien abductions could be accountable. They might have become bored of pestering cultivators with crop circles, and abducting cattle. Aliens and Atlantis however, do not explain the spottings of ghost ships.

Time rifts are also believed to be responsible for disappearances, mechanical breakdowns as well as the appearance in the form of ghost vessels. I'm not knowledgeable the details of time rifts to disprove this, but these phenomena are not explained.

Fig . 3 : Avengers aircrafts

2-5-2 : SCIENTIFIC/NATURAL EXPLAINATION

There have been speculations that there exist methane gas pockets that are lit by lightning, or perhaps an electric spark. Methane does exist similar to this throughout the globe naturally, and there hasn't been similar incident. At the very least, there haven't been any incidents that are attributed to methane explosions. Methane is dispersed very quickly when it enters the air, which makes it less risky.

Others suggest that there are some rogue tides, which can occur however this isn't the reason for the disappearances of planes. It doesn't even explain the reason why there isn't any debris. or stories such as the Ellen Austin's story, in which the cargo was intact and the vessel was safe to sail.

2-5-3 : THERE'S NO Mystery

This area of ocean has been highly frequented, and planes and ships will disappear in the coming years. However, there is no statistically significant anomaly in the disappearances within this region. Certain planes and ships who claim to have disappeared in the Bermuda Triangle are not real or the facts surrounding disappearances are either invented or exaggerated.

It is believed that the U.S. Navy and Coast Guard are not aware of that the Bermuda Triangle as a threat. It is also worth noting that the U.S. Board of Geographic Names is not even acknowledging Bermuda Triangle as a geographical location. Bermuda Triangle as a geographic area.

There are numerous tropical storms that are affecting the region and violent, rapid changes in weather caused by the Gulf Stream, which would cause sinking of ships, destroy planes, and then wash it across the Gulf Stream, where debris may be washed up so far that no one can connect it to lost aircrafts or ships. But even the NOAA states that there is evidence that magnetic compasses are pointing to the true North in the opposite direction to magnetic North However, there is no explanation for this .

Fig . 2 - Depiction of a dance-related epidemic which occurred in 1564. 2-5-3-1 : In the summer of 1518, a woman started dancing at Strasbourg, Alsace (now modern-day France) of the Holy Roman Empire

There are sources that do not give her a name however, others refer to the woman as Frau Troffea. The dancer was in the studio for about 4-6 days, where more than 30 people were also dancing with her, mostly women of the ages of 18 to 24. In July, at the time of the July 31st there was a report that 400 to 400 people joined her. The bishop, magistrate and doctors from the local area attempted to stop the dance. Evidently, they recommended additional dancing as a remedy for the manic dance. The sources of the time do not include deaths caused by dancing, however later sources report deaths due to strokes, heart attacks as well as exhaustion and dehydration.

Fig . 2-5: Painting of dancing madness among peasants. 2-6 : Mysterious

What was the reason for hundreds of people dancing for days with no reason? According to reports, they weren't in a state of convulsion, but dancing with purpose. 2-7: How did the first woman survive?

It is reported that she danced for about 4-6 days at minimum, however she could be dead of dehydration within three days.

* Dancing for all night is also beyond the endurance of even the most elite athletes. Why did so many of them join her?

* If one woman loses her head, then what might make the other women take the same action?

Fig . 2-6: Ergot in wheat.

2-8: ERGOT POISONING

Ergot is a type of mold that develops on rye and can trigger hallucinations and spasms and tremors. This is the most frequently cited causes of the dance-related plague. Some point to spasms and tremors as being interpreted as dancing but contemporaneous evidence is clear the cause was dance not spasms. If all of the people in the area were afflicted with Ergot poisoning the effects are different for everyone. It isn't likely that everyone would react by dancing around in the same way.

Also, it is important to note that there were other dance-related famines throughout history.

2-8-1: IT'S MYTHICAL

It could be that all of the dance plagues that are mentioned in the past were myths meant to give lessons about sin. All of them were believed to have occurred in modern-day France and Germany specifically in German-speaking regions.

In 1021 CE in 1021 CE, Koelbigk in the city of Koelbigk, there were people "dancing in the ring of sin" in the middle of an evening church service on Christmas Eve. Evidently, the priest, angry at the interruption, cursed the people to dance for one year, up to Christmas Eve. They were able to dance for one year. It's not clear if this is a fairy tale or a description of a real-life incident that has morphed into myth.

2-8-2: In Erfurt 1247 CE 200 people were dancing on the bridge, which fell and the water gushed over them.

In 1347 in 1347, in 1347, a "terrible desire" to dance took over Western Germany, the Low Country as well as Northeastern France. The stories seem to have consequences for this type of dancing that could spell the subject of a curse or with death. It is possible that they were created or embellished to shield people, specifically the women who are frequently dancing in the tales and from misbehavior.Maybe these dance-related calamities were never even real.

But, there is a well-documented case from the past that could shed some more light on this issue.

2-9: STRESS-INDUCED PSYCHOSIS

Tanganyika on the 30th of January 1962, girls from an boarding school run by missionaries in Kashasha started to laugh. The first incident was with three girls who chuckled at the top of their lungs. The incident spread throughout the school in a blaze of laughter, and by the time almost all of the students who attended in the class were laughing out loud at different times for a diverse time period - some for just only a few hours, and others more than two weeks. The only ones affected were the students and it did not affect the instructors. School was forced be closed for a short period on March 18th due to the incessant laughter that was affecting the students. The outbreak was then spread to nearby Nshamba which is where the students suffering from this condition resided. Around 200 residents most of them young, were afflicted by the inexplicably loud laughter. The school was attempting to reopen but was forced to shut down because of the outbreak. The outbreak was then spread across other institutions. The closure of 14 schools was a huge blow and over 1,000 were affected by the raucous laughter. It lasted for 18 months.

Let's look at the dancing epidemic in 1518. It was a major problem for young women, just like the epidemic of laughter.

The area had been hit with an earlier hunger crisis. People were forced to begging to survive. Many people died due to hunger.

Many were dying of small pox epidemics and Syphilis.

The local population was aware about a legend in the church of Saint. Vitus, who would cause a convulsive plague of dances to those who had did him wrong.

Mass Psychogenic Illness is a type of "mass hyperstimulation" that is caused by stress on a large number of people, usually for those with low status and/or without power. The issue is whether it is affecting Tanganyikan girls attending the missionary school, dealing with cultural dissonance, the country's recently gained independence "conversion reaction" as well as young girls who lived in the midst of famine or epidemics of disease and the challenges that young women faced in the middle ages of Europe.

Fig . 2-7 : Illustration of Jack the Ripper in 1888. 2-10: Whitechapel was one of the districts located in the East End of London in 1888.

It was overcrowded, impoverished and suffered from an endemic problem of alcoholism, robbery and even violence. There was an area where immigrants from poor backgrounds lived in. Women living there were often forced to prostitute to earn a living. It is important to note that in the past the act of prostitution was not considered illegal. Socially it was considered to be the lowest of the lowest. Prostitutes were thought to be the lowest level of society. However the fact that there were around 1,200 prostitutes who were active in Whitechapel according to contemporaneous information from the London Metropolitan Police Service (1888). Thus, it appears that despite the fact that the society was averse to treating them as lepers there was a huge market for these women.

Whitechapel was referred to as Whitechapel was referred to as a "den of violence and immorality." The housing and work in Whitechapel was a mess and it was getting worse. More than half of the children perished before the age of 5. Given the ferocity of Whitechapel it is likely that a body of dead is not a rare sighting. However the fact that at least five murders at Whitechapel were so horrific, they could be shocking even the most ardent of the Whitechapel residents. Fig . 2-8: Police Illustrated News, Sept. 8, 1888 with the story of an assassination of Mary Ann Nichols.

2-10-1: Five to eleven murders of women perpetrated by one person between 1888 and 1891 remain unsolved as of today.

The murders may be traced to one individual however, there are many disputes. This time we'll only talk on the confirmed five murder victims by the murderer who is known throughout the history of "Jack the Ripper."

On the 31st of August in 1888, a carter saw the naked body of a young lady. He was frozen until he could hear the footsteps of a different person approaching the scene - a second carter. He yelled: "come and look over here. There's an unidentified female lying in the ground." Two carters attempted to look for warning signs of life, but were unable to determine if the woman was drunk or dead. The first said she was dead. The second thought the woman was alive and advised putting her in a chair. The first declined. The skirts were tied around her waist, and so after deciding that they would be late to work if they decided to collect police, they threw her skirts off and set ahead. They claimed that they would notify the first police officer they met while on their way. However, a police officer was able to locate her shortly after the men quit the location..

2-10-2: The body was that of Mary Nichols, whose throat was cut so deeply that she was close to being killed.

Her abdomen was cut. Nichols had been a prostitute living in Whitechapel and was in search of a buyer so that she could pay the cost of lodging for the night, according to her most recent appearance.

The murders were then followed by the deaths Annie Chapman, Elizabeth Stride, Catherine Eddowes, and Mary Kelly. They were all known prostitutes with alcohol problems, with Mary Kelly to a much less extent. She was the smallest and was the one least damaged by age and illness. She was an occasional prostitute, according to people that knew her. Everyone was slit in the throat. Elizabeth Stride was the only person who was not injured, and it is believed that the murderer was interrupted during the slaying.

2-11: Suspects

The police believe that he was a local who had the medical expertise or expertise to cut up the human body, and even eliminate organs. There are more than 100 suspects in the case of The Jack-the-Ripper. More than 300 people from the vicinity of Whitechapel were examined. Yet, the mystery remains.

Who did Jack the Ripper? The answer is clear according to my opinion, however, we must get rid of the suspects we've been using for a while.

2-11-1: PRINCE ALBERT EDWARD

The most outrageous and among the latest suspects are the prince Albert Edward, heir to the throne. The theory is that he conceived an unlucky Catholic woman pregnant, who had a child named Alice and was hidden away by her nanny Mary Kelly.

Fig . 2-9 : Cartoon that criticizes the police's incompetence in the case of September. 22nd 1888

The girl confessed her story to a handful of prostitutes who were in the area. To cover up the scandal, agents working for the crown murdered prostitutes. They also and then accidentally killed Catherine Eddowes, since she frequently was known as Mary Kelly, and then eventually murdered the real nanny in order to conceal the unlegitimate child. Another story claims that this "ladies man" who was father to one child outside of wedlock was a gay man who hated women and could have killed himself.

Who was the person who told this tale? The answer is a descendant from Alice Of course.

We can certainly affirm, given that the fact that Prince Albert Edward was out of the country for two murders and the insaneness of the story it is unlikely that he was Jack the Ripper.

11-2 : MONTAGUE DRUITT

Montague Druitt was a victim of the unlucky feature of being a homosexual person in the year 1888. He was in part the profile that was provided of a man who was spotted with a woman shortly before her death: well-dressed, "jewish-looking," with mustache, and in his 30s. Also, he died between November and December 1888, at which point it was believed that the Ripper went into hiding (if we do not count the deaths that came after) most likely due to suicide after being dismissed from his position as a teacher.

The man who was accused of him was a man named Macnaghten who was involved in the trial in 1889, was not able to make a convincing argument. One reason was that Macnaghten was incorrect regarding a number of facts concerning Druitt including his age and occupation (he taught striving to become barristers, not a doctor, as Macnaghten claimed). 2. Macnaghten said he was the owner of evidence that he could not divulge which implicated Druitt. However, it was never made public or discovered. Druitt had no connection to Whitechapel or any evidence that he was ever there. Even the principal detective on the case was skeptical about that.

"I have all the details of the story. But what exactly does it relate to? It's as simple as this. Shortly after the crime of Whitechapel an unidentified doctorwas found in the Thames However, there is nothing beyond the fact that he was discovered at that time to implicate the doctor."

-"Inspector Abberline

211-3 : OTHERS

A man who was believed to be the husband of the victim cut his throat with a knife and committed suicide. This was believed to be evidence that there was a possibility that he was the Ripper.

Somebody claimed they had discovered journal entries from James Maybrick, who confessed in it to be Jack the Ripper. This was later discovered to be an espionage by the person who discovered it. However, he later claimed that it was authentic afterward. So who is to say?

The 2-11-3-1 case : Carl Feigenbaum apparently confessed to being Jack the Ripper, saying he had an inexplicably strong desire to murder and disfigure women

The execution took place in the U.S. after he cut the throat of a woman. might be in London in the past? There's no evidence to suggest there is any evidence that he did, however there was a possibility that he was a seaman in Europe in the time of the murders. Anyone who was in London (or perhaps not, given that the fact that Prince Albert Edward was accused of the murders even though they were out of London) during the period could be Jack the Ripper.

To my mind, it seems fairly simple. What is it that this single curator at a museum of history located in Cleveland, TN managed to determine as being Jack the Ripper after 130 years of detectives and historians were unable to?

1-1-4 : CHARLES CROSS

It was the man who discovered the first victim. The carter. Although the writer of this site is utterly dismissive of evidence against Cross, they have the ability to build a case. The opening and the closing statement are both mocking about Cross as being the Ripper

However, the evidence presented provides a convincing argument.

When I first started to read the tale about Mary Nichols, as soon when I read the account of the carter, I thought "he was the one who did this." Based on the testimony of the other carter Cross was standing in the same spot as the woman but Cross offered a contradictory account. The second carter believed the woman was alive and was trying to prop her up. Cross believed it was over and did not want to. If they'd tried to hold her and then reveal the wound that nearly killed her. The second witness said that "he stated that the police would have called an officer but was behind in time. I was also behind in time." Cross also gave his false name and address to police (though Cross provided his actual location of work and address). It was reported that he was known to be a deceitful liar. His real name was Lechmere.

2-11-4-1 : The officer who found the body after the two carters left was an officer with a beat who was doing rounds

He was on the road at around 3:15 A.M. about 30 minutes before he spotted her, and she wasn't there. We have a 30 minutes time frame for the execution. The second carter claimed they found her and Cross in the 3rd quarter of three forty A.M. when questioned later. The policeman discovered her at 3:45. A doctor is on the scene at around four A.M. and states that she was not dead for longer than 30 minutes.

If we take the medical evidence from 1888 regarding the time of death, and the estimated the time of death of the living at around four A.M., that means Mary Nichols was murdered between 3:40 and 3:40 am. It would have been necessary for her to be slit in the throat to cause an immediate death. The injury on her abdominal area was said to take just five minutes to perform.

He was a local guy who delivered meats to Pickfords So he would not have been inappropriate if he was covered in bloodstains. He could have had a knowledge of butchery from this. It's not clear. The route that he traveled through took him to all the murder scenes with the exception of Elizabeth Stride, who was found close to the place where his mother's house was.

There's a great deal of evidence to support his claims (all of it circumstantial). Take the time to study the evidence to see what it's worth, not simply listening to the author's remark about his lack of credibility, and then consider what you think. This website could not exist if Jack the Ripper mystery was solved.

2-12: The Truth is that we will never be able to solve one of these Mysteries

It's not that easy. It's impossible to say if I'm 100% right, even though I'm a skeptical person who is prone to sticking to Occam's razor , which is the most straightforward solution is typically the best one. There are patterns being observed throughout Bermuda Triangle. Bermuda Triangle because human brains are wired to detect patterns. Dancing plagues are the result of mass hysteria that affect those who are marginalized. Charles Cross got caught murdering Mary Nichols so his excuse was that he had found the body.

Researchers make key discoveries in Bermuda Triangle:Wreckage "has an interesting story that needs telling'.

An upcoming History Channel documentary reveals an significant discovery in a 76 year-old mystery involving five planes and 14 airmen that vanished during the Bermuda Triangle.

The 2-12-1 mystery that's been lingering for more than 76 years in an fabled region that sailors and pilots have claimed to have supernatural powers that we aren't able to comprehend.

On December. 5th in 1945, 14 pilots piloting 5 World War II torpedo bombers known as Avengers left Naval Air Station Fort Lauderdale in a routine flight training mission across the Bermuda Triangle and were never ever seen again. There was a rumor that the U.S. Navy even sent an Martin Mariner aircraft to search to search for the aircraft that was missing and the crew of 13 disappeared.A fresh investigation of the scientific evidence surrounding the mystery surrounding the disappearance of this aircraft is the subject on the History Channel documentary "History's Greatest Mysteries" with narration by Laurence Fishburne, that will air in the coming week.

Kerry Sanders got a preview of the documentary today Tuesday, when the lead underwater explorer of the mission revealed the findings of the year-long mission of scientific exploration into Bermuda Triangle. Bermuda Triangle, an area that lies off Florida's coast. Florida which extends from southeast towards Puerto Rico and north to Bermuda.

2-13: Bermuda Triangle Mysteries: Supernatural or Science?

"We are looking at this round fragment of wreckage that has teeth that look like the gears" Michael Barnette, the underwater exploration leader tells us during the film. "I'm thinking that this is an Turret. It's a turret. chart. This could be one of the Avenger?"

In reality, it was the remains of an Avenger which raises speculation as to whether or not it's the remains of an Avenger that was part of the mysterious Flight 19 that disappeared in 1945.

"And this is a legitimate concern," Barnette told Sanders on Today. "We don't have the answer yet as most people are unaware the number of planes that are lost on the coast of Florida.

Fig . 2-10: Kerry Sanders

"This could represent one of the Avengers that were in Flight 19, but it is still a story to tell. And when we know what the aircraft is, we can determine the location of Flight 19 isn't." 2-13-1: Muddying the waters can be seen in the way that scientists have discovered Navy documents that suggest the wreckage that was discovered in the documentary could be an alternative crash. Since 1930, over 325 planes and over 1,200 ships have gone missing in crashes, sinks or crashed in the Bermuda Triangle, which is an area that is roughly as large as Alaska.

Sailors and pilots have often speculated about the possibility that Bermuda Triangle contains inexplicable forces which could indicate the existence of aliens and that Barnette Barnette does not believe.

He believes that the wreckage from Flight 19 is out there however, he does not believe that the ship crashed because of any reason straight from "Close Close Encounters: Third Kind."

"Not anything," he told Sanders. "I place it alongside the Easter bunny as well as the tooth fairy."

Bermuda Triangle Bermuda Triangle is one of the most popular mysteries of our time. In this course we'll look at the background of this legend, and then see the ways that scientists have attempted to understand it.

2-14: The Bermuda Triangle

Its mysteries about the sea have intrigued the people for thousands of years. The magnetism of the ocean, its dangers, as well as the treasures of different treasures that lie within it are always intriguing. There are few things that are as controversial as the mystery of disappearances of human beings to the oceans. The ancient sailors believed that these disappearances were due to gods, monsters and spirits. Since then, modern scientists and sailors have come to see the sea's dangers as natural and completely explainable...mostly.

2-14-1: The Bermuda Triangle is a roughly 500,000 square mile area of the Caribbean situated within Bermuda, Florida, and Puerto Rico

The name was initially used by journalist Vincent Gaddis in 1964, the region has been attracting attention for a long time. However, there has been numerous mysterious disappearances that have occurred within the Bermuda Triangle. Aircrafts and ships disappeared and were not found. What's happening with the Bermuda Triangle? Perhaps, the oceans have a few mysteries to be solved.

Chapter 8: Bermuda Triangle Theories And Counter-Theories

When the author Vincent Gaddis coined the phrase "Bermuda Triangle" in the 1964 issue of a magazine there were other mysterious incidents that had been reported in the area which included three passenger planes which crashed despite sending "all's perfectly" messages. Charles Berlitz, whose grandfather was the founder of the Berlitz language schools, ignited the legend further in 1974 by writing an amazing book on the legend. Since since then, scores of fellow writers of the paranormal have blamed the supposed danger on anything including aliens Atlantis as well as sea creatures to time-warps and reverse gravity fields. However, more science-based theorists have suggested waterspouts, magnetic anomalies or massive explosions of methane gas that have come from the bottom of the ocean.

Fig. 2-17: U.S. Coast Guard

2-21 : In all likelihood however, there is no theory that will solve the mystery

According to one skeptic that trying to discover the common reason for each Bermuda Triangle disappearance is no more sensible than trying to discover an underlying cause of every car accident in Arizona. Furthermore, while reefs, storms and those of the Gulf Stream can cause navigational issues the maritime insurance giant Lloyd's of London does not consider Bermuda Triangle as a Bermuda Triangle as an especially risky area. The same is the case for the U.S. Coast Guard, that says: "In a review of several losses of vessels and aircraft within the region over the decades, there has been anything that suggests that the casualties resulted from anything other than physical factors. The cause of the loss has never been discovered."

2. The Encyclopaedia Britannica

3. A&E Television Networks, October 13 2021

3: Famous Events that occurred in the Bermuda Triangle

The time the U.S.S. Cyclops was unable to connect someplace north of Barbados It was among the top viewed instances of the perplexing dangers lurking in the Bermuda Triangle.

A Navy's biggest fuel vessels The Cyclops has been last seen the day of this event on Mar. 4, 1918, as it stopped at the West Indies on its way from Brazil to Baltimore with 10,000 tons of manganese ore to be used in the production of ammunition. The ship did not make it to Baltimore and neither did any of its passengers of 300 and crew members.

Fig . 3-1: The USS Cyclops was lost in Bermuda in 1918. APIC / Getty Images

Despite a long-running search there was no trace discovered of the vessel, and Naval investigators could not find an exact reason for the ship's disappearance.

The thing that made it more intriguing According to a current New York Times account, was the fact that the captain did not send a distress signal and neither did any of the crew respond to radio messages from thousands of American ships that were in the vicinity.

Additionally the storms were not that were strong enough for the Cyclops to sink According to the Times the newspaper, which then went on to suggest that the vessel could be the target of German U-boats or mines. As per the Naval History and Heritage Command One magazine of the time said that a huge Octopus "risen from the ocean and encircled the ship's hull with its tentacles and then dragged it down to its bottom."

3-1: The Navy However, it discounted the possibility of German or giant octopus-sized attacks

The door is open to further strange speculations as the Cyclops added to the list of over 100 planes and ships to disappear under bizarre conditions in the triangular area which is bordered roughly with Bermuda, Miami and Puerto Rico.

Although Bermuda Triangle was a popular topic of discussion, Bermuda Triangle became a cultural fixation in between the years 1950 and 1960, it's by recently been extensively dismissed. Its image as a sort of black hole in the earth suffers every time a disappearing vessel or plane reappears.

3-2 : Even though there's no sign of the Cyclops however, there's at the very least an alternative explanation

It focuses on an eccentric captain than Ahab and who was known to "pacing the quarterdeck in an apron as well as a cane, and underneaths," and against whom certain members of his crew had attempted to revolt before they arrived in Barbados according to the Navy. According to the book by Gian Quasar Distant Horizons The U.S. Consul in Barbados wrote to the State Department following the ship's disappearance, stating that the captain seemed to be a snobby and unpopular figure among his colleagues, and that , in the process of putting down the mutiny that had occurred the captain had confined the members of his team, and even executed one.

"While there is no definitive reasons, I am afraid of fate more than sinking" Consul wrote "though it could be rooted in the instinctive hatred I feel towards the master." 3-3 : The Mystery of Bermuda Triangle Remains One

As the skeptical scientists were about to offer an explanation that seemed reasonable the myth about Bermuda Triangle was revealed. Bermuda Triangle today was declared to be alive and even causing a lot of trouble on along the coastline of South Florida.

The underwater explorers who revealed in the last month that they may have found five Navy planes that mysteriously disappeared in 1945, setting a base for the myth of an underwater craft-swallowing Caribbean twilight zone, stated that after closer inspection the planes they discovered were not identical to the legendary "Flight 19."

"The Bermuda Triangle, I'm worried about, if you're looking to uncover the mysteries it's probably alive and healthier than it was in the past," said Graham S. Hawkes who was the British engineer who was on the exploration ship that was spotted aboard the Avenger aircraft on May 8 while searching for sunken treasure.

With a mix of sadness and joy the He expressed a mixture of sadness and relief. Hawkes said at a press briefing that in four out of five instances the tail numbers of the planes his team located did not match those of the aircraft that was lost. It happened to be the plane with "28" -the same number that was written on the lead aircraft -it was the one the explorers first spotted according to him. They later discovered that the Navy frequently reused their tail number from the aircraft lost.

Fig . 3. digital copy of an article that was part of The Times's archive for print prior to the introduction of the online publication in.

To keep these articles in the way they first were published, The Times does not modify, or even update them.

Sometimes the digitization process can introduce transcription errors , or other problems We are always trying to to improve the archives.

On close passes of the submerged planes advanced remote camera, which operates directly from the Mr. Hawkes's boat Deep See Deep See, could not find serial numbers for any planes. However, the type of model indicated that the majority of planes had been built prior to the crash on Dec. 5th, 1945.

3-4: How the five Avengers were clustered within the 1.2-nautical mile radius

resting upright and mostly unharmed with a 550-750 foot depth below the surface and 550 to 750 feet below the surface, Mr. Hawkes and his crew were still speculating. However, he assured the assembled media, "You can discount aliens."

Ted Darcy, a marine archeologist who looked at videotapes from the Deep See's discovery believes that a naval airbase located in Fort Lauderdale had used an area that was near the spot which the planes were located for dropping torpedos at low altitude. The researchers believed that each plane could have crashed for a long period of time as they made exercises towards the location of the target.

The "Lost Patrol,"" according to what this squadron is known by a group of investigators from pulp-paperbacks began their journey from the former Fort Lauderdale Naval Air Station in the city's current international airport in a regular three-hour training mission. In the event of bad weather the pilot who was leading the team lost his bearings, believing they were in an area called the Gulf of Mexico. The planes were apparently flying to the east, and then further to the Atlantic. The commander finally instructed the planes to drop in a row when they first was running low on fuel. Their radio signals were cut off. In spite of a search covering 250,000 square miles The 14 flyers weren't heard of ever again.

3-4 : The Mystery was only beginning there

Inundated by the reports of radios dead, broken compasses and flying objects that were not identified (not to forget disappearances of hundreds of vessels and planes) the region of Miami, Puerto Rico and Bermuda became known to those who believe in the existence that was ruled by supernatural powers. At at least 139 of the World War II vintage Avengers were taken away off along the Florida coast.

Although newspapers and writers continue to promote the idea of a vast oceans, scientists have been saying for decades that there's no evidence to support it.

The Mr. Hawkes and his colleagues stated that they were happy to continue their quest to search through 1000 square miles on ocean floor in search of Spanish galleons, as well as other interesting or valuable wrecks.

Following a torrent in media scrutiny, an avalanche of offers from film and TV producers, as well as an unofficial battle with the Navy They declared that they weren't sure they were going to locate additional aircraft.

"If we find five additional planes," said Mr. Hawkes declared, "I'm not sure we'll inform anyone."

3- 6 3

1. David Crookes , All About Space magazine July 08th 2020
2. Tim Golden, June 5, 1991
3. JENNIFER LATSON , 4 MARCH 2015
4. Scott Stump, Aug. 31, 2021
5. The New York Times Archives

Fig . 3-3: The Van Allen Probes (VAP) was launched in 2012 and continued to operate for seven years in order to gain a better understanding of the radiation belts of Earth. (Image Cr: NASA) 3-7 People, planes and ships have been known to vanish without explanation in a region in the North Atlantic Ocean known as the Bermuda Triangle.

Bermuda Triangle

Could it be the work of extraterrestrials or force-pulling objects beneath the sea, or even a connection to the mythical lost city Atlantis? Could it be the result of bad conditions, Human error, or excessive traffic in the region?

It's hard to say for sure however, more than 50 aircrafts and ships disappeared since the middle of the 19th century. It's not more than any other area that is well-travelled in the ocean, yet the conspiracy theories persist.

If we gaze up into the sky, we may see something similar to"the "Bermuda triangle of space."

This vast space over Earth is known to cause havoc to spacecraft that enter the region. Spacecraft aren't disappearing into the void However, the disturbance caused is still serious and can pose a risk to both astronauts and equipment.

3-7-1: The Bermuda Triangle of space lies over the South Atlantic, stretching from Chile to Zimbabwe

It's located in the area where the outer Van Allen radiation belt comes closest to the Earth's surface. Earth is home to two Van Allen belts, which are two doughnut-shaped rings made of charged particles which surround our planet. which are held together by the Earth's magnetic field. The inner portion is made up predominantly of protons that are high energy, and the outer one is mostly electrons. Since the belts hold the particles that shoot out from the surface of sun, they are responsible for protecting the planet's surface against harmful radiation.

3-7-2 : At the point in 3-7-2: In the Bermuda Triangle of space, or the South Atlantic Anomaly (SAA) in the official terms Earth's magnetic field is extremely weak.

The particles of cosmic rays from the sun aren't being restricted to the same degree like they are elsewhere on the earth. In the end, solar rays can travel closer than 200 km (124 miles) to Earth's surface. The higher intensity of solar radiation causes an increased flow of powerful particles within this region.

"I'm not a fan of the name, but in this region the lower geomagnetic field intensity will eventually result in higher vulnerability of satellites to intense particles to the point where spacecraft damage can be experienced as they travel through the region," said John Tarduno who is a professor of geophysics in the University of Rochester. "The lower intensity of the magnetic field permits Earth's radiation belttechnically, the inner belt to move closer to Earth's surface" Tarduno told All About Space. "Thus satellites traveling across this area will be exposed to more radiation, until damage may be caused. Consider an electric discharge or arc. When there is more radiation coming in the satellite could become charged, and the resulting arches can cause severe harm."

3-8 : What happens with astronauts and spacecrafts within the SAA?

Typically, the Van Allen belts stretch at an altitude between 1,000 to 60,000 kilometers (620 to 37,000 miles) over the Earth's surface. The relatively low elevation of the radiation hotspot however, places it inside the orbit of satellites that are bombarded by protons with the energy in excess of 10,000,000 electron volts (eV) at an average of 3000 "hits" for every square centimeter every second.

The spacecraft's onboard electronics. This hinders the performance of these satellites and makes it necessary for space agencies as well as others operating satellites to shut the systems down. This is also true to Hubble. Hubble telescope which travels over the SAA 10 times daily and spends a decent 15 percent of its time in the SAA.

Hubble cannot collect high-frequency data in these times This isn't the best solution however it is necessary.

All About Space magazine takes readers on an amazing voyage through the space system, and further starting with the amazing spacecraft and technology that allow us to go into space, all the way to the intricate world of the science of space.

Failure to take the necessary precautions when shutting down the spacecraft will probably result in system failure , something astronauts have seen before when computers were installed on craft flying close to the SAA. The only way to prevent this is to implement measures of protection. "Putting equipment in a'safe mode' indicates that operations that are more prone to radiation are slowed down," Tarduno said.

3-8-1 : the more complicated electronic circuits have become more complex, the greater potential is for issues to arise.

Any satellites using this system of tracking microwaves DORIS -that stands for Doppler orbitography as well as Radiopositioning Integrated by SatelliteFor instance, you can see the resulting shift in Oscillator onboard frequency.

Damage caused by SAA can be extremely expensive, as was evident by the time the region caused an Japanese satellite Hitomi into Earth. Hitomi is also known as ASTRO-H. It was launched from the Japan Aerospace Exploration Agency (JAXA) to investigate extremely active processes that occur in the universe. Within a month of the launch in February the spacecraft's operators lost contact with the satellite and it split into several pieces. Experts later found out that the issue resulted from the satellite's internal reference units (a kind that is a motion sensor) showing a spin that was 21.7 degree per hour, when the spacecraft was actually steady. The attitude control system tried to stop the non-existent spin, a series of events led it to fail.

3-8-2: Had the operators could have detected the error at the time of its detection they could have rectified it.

It happened when the satellite was in the SAA thus the communication was cut off.

There is also the possibility that the massive radiation dose influenced the electronic components. Whatever the case the tragic incident cost JAXA around $273 million, in addition to three years of compiled research.

Astronauts may be in the grip of SAA as well. Many have reported seeing strange white lights flashing in front of their eyes. Steps are being taken to safeguard astronauts aboard the International Space Station (ISS). A strong shield is installed over the most frequent used areas of the ISS like the gallery as well as the sleeping quarters in order to minimize exposure to radiation astronauts are exposed. Astronauts also carry dosimeters which measure the amount of exposure they receive to ionizing radiation in real-time, and issue a warning in the event that they exceed dangerous levels. 3-9 : What is the cause of the SAA?

Why is the magnetic field weaker over that of the South Atlantic? This is due to the shape of the Earth that isn't entirely round. The Earth is slightly rounded in the middle and its magnetic dipole field off from its central point by approximately 500km (300 miles). The area where the dip is the cosmic rays and charged particles are closer to Earth's surface , and offer less protection against interplanetary radiation. However the magnetic bubble keeps solar winds from reaching Earth's surface.

Fig. 3-4: How the South Atlantic Anomaly (SAA) is made. (Image Cr: Getty) 3-9-1 The field of magnetic energy is maintained by a dynamo procedure that is caused by the flow of liquid metal that flows through Earth's core, which generates electric currents.

As the planet spins around its orbit, the tense movement of charged, molten matter is what creates the magnetic field. It creates the south and north poles that are visible from the surface. However, the poles aren't always permanent since the Earth's magnetic field changes constantly, becoming more and less when it moves.

Presently it is apparent that the field of magnetic energy reducing within the SAA This means that the area is expanding.

Tarduno and his coworkers are studying the duration of time the SAA has been in operation. They discovered an unmatched geological source in Africa that reveal what the the magnetic field of Earth looked like in the past, thousands of years.

Bantu farmer who lived within the Limpopo River Valley in Africa 1000 years ago, would engage in the ritual of cleansing that included burning their homes in times of drought to get their lives back on track and to encourage rain.

The process resulted in release of magnetic minerals within the clay, which will be aligned with the Earth's magnetic field, before cooling. This gave Tarduno and his team with stunning images of the magnetic field at the time.

"We observed something different in the core-mantle boundary beneath Africa," Tarduno

They also said that it could affect the magnetic field of the world. The team discovered evidence that suggests the SAA is the most active manifestation of a regular phenomenon.

"Under Africa, at the core-mantle border, which is just over the iron core that is liquid the field reverses. This is known as the reversed flux patch" Tarduno said. "It This patch appears to be responsible for the majority of the weak field as well as it is also responsible for the SAA." Scientists have also researched whether this could mean that it is set to change direction, however studies that are based on observations from the last fifty years suggest that the SAA isn't a sign of this.

Fig . 3: An artist's rendering that shows the proton-dominated, inner belt (red) and the outer belt, composed from electrons (blue). (Image Cr: NASA) 3-10 : The SAA expansion will mean to Earthlings in space and for space-travel

Additional research has also examined the degree of danger that radiation in the SAA might be at various levels. This is vital since the increasing region of SAA could not only lead to more issues with computers and other electronic devices in Earth however, it may also cause an increase in the incidence of cancer.

Riccardo Campana from Riccardo Campana at the National Institute for Astrophysics in Bologna, Italy, analyzed radiation data from the satellite of Italy-Dutch for Astronomy using X-rays BeppoSAX that often traveled through the lower portion of the SAA between 1996 to 2003. The results showed that radiation levels were lower in the lower layers of SAA than in the higher layers.

3-10-1 : However 3-10-1: As the European Space Agency points out that the magnetic field in this region has diminished by about 15 percent of its strength over the last 150 years.

Prior to 1994 the north pole of the magnetic north was moving at about 10 kilometers (6.2 miles) annually, however it has increased to approximately 65km (40 miles) annually since 2001. Can the magnetic field disappear completely and leave Earth completely open to radiation?

"This is not a matter of concern for billions of years in the future," Tarduno said. "Even in times of magnetic reversals there is an electromagnetic field, though less powerful and more complicated in its structure as compared to the present.

"The question now concerns whether or not we're actually in the beginning stages of a magnetic reverse. The dramatic decline in the strength of the dipole field in the last 160 years as well as the pattern of decline provide some evidence to consider this as an option, however the short period of the observed decrease places this in the realm of speculation."

At present, the primary focus is on exploration of space, especially because the number of spacecraft and satellites carrying human beings is likely to rise. Understanding how the SAA does its job is essential because , as it expands at an average at 19.3 kilometers

(12 miles) annually the SAA will be covering a larger area than it currently does.

3-11 : Bermuda Triangle Incidents

This is a constantly changing list that will never be able to meet certain standards of fullness. It is possible to contribute the missing items using reliable sources. The following is a listing that includes incidents which are attributed in popular culture with Bermuda Triangle or Devil's Triangle. Bermuda Triangle or Devil's Triangle.

Chapter 9: Investigation

The U.S. government launched an thorough inquiry into the mysterious disappearance of the team of Deering. There are five departmental offices of the federal governmentfive departments of the government Commerce, Treasury, Justice, Navy, and State- -looked into the matter. Herbert Hoover, then Secretary of Commerce was interested at the discovery that other vessels with different nationalities, most particularly the sulfur freighter Hewitt disappeared within the same location. Though the majority of these vessels were later found to be sailing within the vicinity of several particularly strong hurricanes,

The Hewitt and Deering proved to be moving away from the vicinity of the storm during the time of the storm. The assistant of Hoover, Lawrence Ritchey, was assigned to the investigation. Ritchey attempted to record what transpired on the ship between its last appearance in Cape Lookout and its running on the ground near Diamond Shoals by reading the log books of the Coast Guard lightships stationed in these areas.

After an Italian investigation about the loss of ship Monte San Michele confirmed that there were strong hurricanes in the area there was a mutiny.

Accepted as the reason as the reason Deering incident.

The investigation was concluded in the latter part of 1922 but there was no official decision regarding the incident. 3-15-5: Speculation

There were many stories regarding the incident. At first, it appeared that an outside force was behind that crew's disappearance.

The 11th of April, 1921 an individual from the local fishing community named Christopher Columbus Gray claimed to discover a message hidden in an empty bottle that was floating in the ocean off Buxton Beach in North Carolina; he swiftly transferred it to authorities.

The message's text was in the form of:

DEERING Captured By OIL BOATS BURNING, WHICH LOOK similar to CHASER. Handcuffing CREW OFF EVERYTHING. CREW is hiding everything over the ship, so there is no chance to escape. If you are a FINDER, please notify the Headquarterers Deering.

The handwriting on this letter has been identified to be the handwriting from the engineer of the vessel, Bates and was discovered by his widow, Captain Wormell and the bottle was found to be made in Brazil. This, in conjunction with the observation of an "mysterious" steamer which arrived in Cape Lookout lightship Cape Lookout lightship in the following of the Deering which suggested hostile actions. The lightship's captain tried to contact the steamer's team to transmit the information of the Deering however, the steamer was unable to respond , and the captain was unable to discern the ship's name as the crew had rolled out an unintentional canvas that covered the nameplate.7

The message was also viewed with suspicion as to whether a member of the crew was able to grab hold of pen, paper and bottle to write a letter, then why did he ask to be informed by the company instead of officers or the Coast Guard? Experts in handwriting concluded that the letter was fake and, following more investigation from federal officials, Christopher Gray admitted to the forgery.8Gray was believed to have made the note with the intention that the publicity he could receive from exposing the note would allow him to secure work in Cape Hatteras Light Station. Cape Hatteras light station.

These theories were examined as a possibility by government officials of the U.S. government in its investigation: Hurricanes U.S. government, particularly the Weather Bureau, strongly advocated the existence of a string of devastating storms that were at war throughout the Atlantic as the primary cause for disappearances. However, as mentioned earlier it was clear that it appears that both Deering as well as the Hewitt were not in the route that these hurricanes were heading. However, numerous writers, including Larry Kusche and Richard Winer have noted that the condition of the vessel indicates an orderly and not the panicked evacuation.

Piratery: The Captain O. W. Parker of the United States Marine Shipping Board was certain that piracy was the cause and stated that according to his view, "Piracy without a doubt is still in existence since the time that of Phoenicians". The widow of Captain Wormell was a fervent advocate of this idea. The belief was that pirates were the culprits behind the disappearances, however no proof of this hypothesis was ever discovered and no pirates ever were caught.

Russian/Communist piracy: In an investigation by police at Headquarters of the United Russian Workers Party (a Communist organisation) located in New York City, officers were allegedly able to find documents calling members of the group to take over American ships and transport towards in the Soviet Union. It is widely believed that this could be relevant to

The Deering incident in the year 2000 the Deering incident was a target of hardline anti-communists within the government. But there is no evidence for any evidence that suggests that the planned actions actually were executed.

Rum runners. A comparable theory like the one mentioned above speculates that a group of alcohol smugglers operating out of the Bahamas took over the vessel to use it as an rum-running vessel (this was in the Prohibition period). The Deering was big enough, as per Richard Winer's Ghost Ships, to carry around 1 million dollars of liquor within her cargo. However it's highly unlikely that such a prominent easily identifiable and slow vessel is the ideal destination for criminals. The evidence for this hypothesis has been found.

Conflict: Wormell's reported dispute with his first mate and his derogatory remarks to his crew members while on the trip to Rio de Janeiro suggested that there was something amiss with the Captain and his crew on the journey. Captain Jacobson at Cape Lookout certainly thought it odd. The man who was a passenger on his vessel was not Captain Wormell and he certainly was not an officer, according to all indications. Senator Frederick Hale of Maine advocated this idea, saying it was "a clear incident of the mutiny". The captain's discontent might have certainly led to the crew to resign however it has never been proved.

Paranormal explanation for the disappearance of the crew members on the ship has been discussed by numerous authors who deal with strange phenomena as well as the supernatural. Charles Fort, in his book Lo! (1931) was the first to mention the ship in the "mysterious" context. numerous subsequent writers of sea mysteries have followed. Because this ship was in the region that is generally thought to be part of the Bermuda Triangle, the disappearance of the crew has frequently been linked in this fact.9However the location of the ship's final resting place

(Diamond Shoals) and the last location of sighting and communication (Cape Watchout) are a few hundred miles from the region commonly referred to by the name of"the Bermuda Triangle. There is no evidence of supernatural events associated with the incident has ever been found.

3-15-6 : There was no official explanation to the reason for the missing crew of Carroll A. Deering was ever given

This case has become a favourite of the paranormal as well as Bermuda Triangle hobbyists and has been praised among the amazing maritime mysteries.

It's also possible that the crew of Deering simply walked away from the ship when the vessel sank at Diamond Shoals and, unable to make it back to the shoreline, got swept to sea and destined for death in their tiny open lifeboats.

The moment they Coast Guard boarded the Deering they saw distress signals, which were two red lights in the rigging, were lit.5The steamer Hewitt that was thought to be in the area could have seen distress signals and brought all the personnel of Deering on board. This Hewitt was later destroyed by all hands and it is probable that Deering crew might have been swept away along with it.10

3-15-7 : Artifacts

In April of 2016 the ship's bell as well as the capstan of the Carrol A. Deering were displayed on display at the Graveyard of the Atlantic Museum in Hatteras.2

Flight 19 is the name of a five-strong group of General Motors Eastern Aircraft Division TBM Avenger torpedo bombers that went missing over the Bermuda Triangle on December 5 1945, after having lost contact during an United States Navy overwater navigation training flight that was originating from Naval Air Station Fort Lauderdale, Florida. All 14 airmen aboard the flight went missing and all 13 crew members from the Martin PBM Mariner flying boat which was later launched at Naval Air Station Banana River to look to find Flight 19. A report from Navy investigation team concluded Flight 19's commander Lieutenant. Charles C. Taylor was mistakenly assuming small islands offshore were The Florida Keys after his compasses failed, leading to the plane heading towards open ocean and away from the land. This report later revised to the Navy to be read as "cause not known" to not blame Taylor as the cause of loss for five aircrafts and 14 passengers. The report linked to the destruction of the PBM aircraft on the ground to an explosion mid-air when searching for the plane.

3-16-1: Navigation Training Flight

Flight 19 took part in the routine navigation and training exercise using TBM-type aircraft.1The mission was known as "Navigation problem no. 1" A combination of navigation and bombing which the other flights had finished or had plans to complete the same day.2The pilot of the flight of the flight was United States Navy Lieutenant Charles Carroll Taylor who had approximately 2,500 flight hours in aircraft of this kind as well as his student pilots who each had 300 totalhours, and 60 hours of flight time within the Avenger.2Taylor had just completed an operational tour of combat in the Pacific region as a torpedo bomber pilot aboard the USS Hancock, an aircraft carrier. USS Hancock as well as just been transferred to NAS Miami where he had also served as an TTB (torpedo-bombing aircraft) instructor. The pilots who were students had recently completed additional training missions within the vicinity that the flight was set going to be taking place.2They included U.S. Marine Captains Edward Joseph Powers and George William Stivers, U.S. Marine Second Lieutenant Forrest James Gerber and USN Ensign Joseph Tipton Bossi; their name signs began with "Fox Tare".

Three aircraft were on the aircraft:

*TBM-1Cs (BuNo 45714, "FT3", BuNo 46325, "FT81"; BuNo 73209, "FT117") 1 TBM-1E (BuNo 46094and "FT36");

*One TBM-3 (BuNo 23307"FT28", 'BuNo 23307').

3-16-2 : Each of the aircrafts was an exact copy that was a variant of the Grumman TBF Avenger, built by General Motors' Eastern Aircraft Division under a wartime production license

In the U.S. Navy aircraft designation system that was in use during World War II, Grummanbuilt Avengers were classified as TBF and GM-built aircrafts like those were designated TBM. They were all fully fueled and in the pre-flight check and inspections, it was discovered that they had no clocks. The navigation of the route was designed to help teach dead counting

concepts, that involved calculations, for example the time elapsed. The apparent absence of time-keeping equipment wasn't a issue since the assumption was that each person had a personal timepiece. Start time was 13:45 local time. However the tardiness from Taylor was delayed until 14:10. The weather in NAS Fort Lauderdale was described as "favorable the sea was moderate and rough".2Taylor was in charge of the mission, while an apprentice pilot was assigned the job of leading at the in front.

3-16-3 : Also known as "Naval Air Station Fort Lauderdale, Florida Navigation problem No. 1",3the exercise consisted of three distinct parts

However, the actual flight should be four. After taking off the plane flew at 091deg (almost due east) for 56 miles (64 miles and 100 km) until they reached Hen along with Chickens Shoals where low level bombing was practiced. The flight would continue along that direction for another 67 miles (77 miles (124 km)) before changing to the 346deg course for 73 miles (84 miles 135 km) as they were taking over Grand Bahama island. The next planned turn was to be a direction of 241deg, allowing for 120 Nmi (140 miles or 220 kilometers) towards the end of the course. completed . The Avengers were to turn left and then return to NAS Fort. Lauderdale.2

Fig . 3-12 : Flight 19's planned navigation exercise on the 5th of December 1945.

1. Get off NAS Fort Lauderdale 14:10 on heading 091deg. Drop bombs at Hen as well as Chickens Shoals (B) until around 15:00, then continue on the 091deg heading to 73 nautical miles (140 km)

2. Left turn and head 346deg and fly up to 73 nautical miles (140 kilometers).

3. Left turn and follow the towards 241deg, which will take 120 nautical miles (220 km) to conclude the training in the northern part of NAS Fort Lauderdale.

4. 17:50 radio triangulation determines the flight's location at 50 nautical miles (93 km) of 29degN 79degW . their last known course of with a 270deg elevation.

5. PBM Mariner leaves NAS Banana River 19:27.

6. 19:50 Mariner explodes near 28degN 80degW.

Radio conversations between pilots were heard by the base and other aircraft operating in the vicinity. The bombing practice is believed to have taken place as at around 15:00, the pilot asked and was granted the permission to throw his final bomb.2 forty minutes later, a second flight instructor Lieutenant Robert F. Cox in the FT-74, which was forming together with his group of students to perform the same purpose, received an unknown transmission.3

3-16-4 : A unidentified crew member was questioned by Powers student to read his compass

Powers responded: "I don't know where we are. It's possible that we've gotten lost following that final turn." Cox then broadcast "This is FT74, plane or boat calling Powers, please identify yourself so that someone is able to assist you." The next response, within a short time was a plea from other passengers in the plane for suggestions. FT-74 attempted to try again and the man identified as FT28 (Taylor) was on the screen. "FT-28 This is FT-74. What's your issue?" "Both of my compasses are missing", Taylor replied, "and I'm trying to locate Fort Lauderdale, Florida. I'm over land, but the map is broken. I'm sure that I am located in the Keys but I'm not sure the depth and am not sure what to do to get to Fort Lauderdale. "2

3-16-5: FT-74 informed the NAS that the aircraft was lost. The NAS instructed Taylor to place an awning with sun, and then fly towards the north, along the coast, to Fort Lauderdale

Base operations asked base operations whether the aircraft used by the flight leader had an YG standard (IFF transmitter) that might be used determine the flight's location however, the message was not recognized by FT-28. (Later he would signal to the base operations that his radio was on.) At 16:45, FT-28 broadcasted: "We are heading 030 degrees for 45 minutes, and then we'll take off north to ensure we aren't above the Gulf of Mexico." At this point, there were no bearings made for the flight and IFF was not heard. Taylor was instructed to broadcast on 4805 kHz. The request was not accepted and he was then asked to change to 3000 kHz, which is the frequency for search and rescue. Taylor said"No "I cannot change frequencies. I have to ensure that my planes remain in good condition. "2

3-16-6: At 16:56, Taylor was asked again to switch on his transmitter to YG in the event that he owned one.

He didn't acknowledge it, however, a couple of minutes later, he the flight was advised to "Change direction at 090 degrees (due east)

for 10 minutes." Around the same time, someone on the plane said "Dammit that If we could fly west, we'd be home, head west Dammit. "2This divergence of opinion caused questions as to the reason why students couldn't simply fly towards the West on their own.4It is believed that this may be due to military discipline.4

As the weather got worse the radio communication became infrequent and it was thought that the five aircraft at the time of this report were over 200 miles (230 miles; 370 km) across the ocean east from the Florida peninsula. Taylor broadcasted "We'll travel 270° to the west until we land or run out of fuel" and demanded an inspection of the weather at 17:24. At 17:50, several radio stations were triangulating Flight 19's location to be within a 100-nmi (120 miles or 190 km) area of 29degN 79degW. Flight 19 was north of the Bahamas and just in central Florida however, no one had transmitted the information on an open repeated basis. In 18:04 Taylor broadcast to Flight 19 "Holding 270. We didn't go far enough to the east, so it's probably best to change direction and fly back to the east". The weather was getting worse and the sun was set. Around 18:20,

Taylor's final message came in. (It was also stated that Taylor's last message arrived at 19:04.)5He was reported to have said "All planes are shut close ... they'll need to abandon the plane unless we land ... at the point that the first plane's weight drops below 10 gallons. We all descend together. "12

3-16-7 : PBM-5 (Bureau Number 59225)

When it became clear that the flight was not found air bases, aircraft, as well as merchant ships received alerts. The Consolidated PBY Catalina departed after 18:00 to find Flight 19 and guide them back to the airport if found. At night two Martin PBM Mariner flying boats planned for their own training flight were diverted for square pattern searches within the region to the west of 29degN and 79degW. US Navy Squadron of Training. 497PBM-5 BuNo 59225 left in 19:27 at Naval Air Station Banana River(now Patrick Space Force Base) It was called for a routine radio call at 19:30, and never heard from again.2

Fig . 3-13: A Martin PBM-5 Mariner similar to BuNo 59225.6

At 21:15 the tanker SS Gaines Mills reported it saw flames coming caused by an apparent blast soaring 100 feet (30 meters) high, and burned for 10 mins at 28.59degN 80.25degW.

Captain Shonna Stanley reported that she was unsuccessfully looking for survivors within the oil as well as aviation fuel. The escort ship USS Solomons also reported losing radar contact with an aircraft in the same place and time.2

3-16-8 : Investigation

An 500-page Navy board of inquiry report, published a few weeks later contained a number of observations:

The flight leader, Lieutenant. Charles C. Taylor had believed, incorrectly, that the tiny islands he crossed were part of the Florida Keys and that his flight passed over the Gulf of Mexico, and that heading north would bring these islands back to Florida. It was found out that Taylor had passed through the Bahamas according to the schedule and actually led his flight towards the northeast across the Atlantic. The report also noted that some subordinate officers were likely to know their exact location as indicated by radio signals which stated that flying west would lead to reaching the mainland.

* Taylor wasn't at fault since the compasses had stopped working. This loss to PBM-5 BuNo 592225 was blamed on an explosion.3

The report was then amended "cause unidentified" to reflect a cause unknown Navy after Taylor's mother claimed that the Navy had been unfairly blaming Taylor's son for the loss of five planes and 14 soldiers, even though the Navy did not have any aircrafts or bodies as evidence.8

3-16-9 : If Flight 19 actually been where Taylor believed it was the plane would have reached land with the Florida coastline in less than 20 minutes.

Depending on how low they depended on how far down they. However, a subsequent analysis of the event revealed that the islands that were visible to Taylor could have been the Bahamas and were located well north of the Keys as well as the fact that Flight 19 was exactly where it was supposed to be. The investigation board discovered that due to the conviction that he was on an initial course towards Florida, Taylor actually guided the plane further north and then out into the ocean. In addition, it was common known of NAS Fort Lauderdale that if the pilot were to get disorientated in this area, they would be required, they would be required to fly with a heading of at least 270deg (due to the west). When the plane was actually turning west, they'd been too far out at sea they'd already exceeded their aircraft's endurance to fuel.

The combination of poor weather conditions, as well as the characteristics of the Avenger1 meant there was little chance of rescue even if they managed to stay on the water.

3-16-10: It is possible that Taylor has strayed too far from Gorda Cay and instead reached another land mass located in southwestern Abaco Islands

He continued to the to the northwest in the direction he had was planned. He had hoped to see that Grand Bahama Island lying in the distance in front of him, as he had expected. However, he spotted an island on his right which was the northern portion of Abaco Island. As if this landmass to his right was Grand Bahama Island and his compasses was out of alignment so he set his direction to what he thought was southwest to go straight back towards Fort Lauderdale. In reality, however, the course shifted north, to the northwest, towards the open ocean.

To add further confusion, Taylor came across an array of islands to the to the north of Abaco Island, which appear like Key West Islands. Key West Islands. The control tower advised Taylor's team to fly west to take them to the island that is Florida eventually. Taylor took off for what he believed would be the west but actually was northwestern, nearly parallel to Florida.

3-16-11 : After attempting that for a few days and seeing no sign of land, Taylor decided that it was impossible to fly this far west , and still not be able to reach Florida

He was convinced that he could be in the vicinity of his home in the Key West Islands. Following was an array of intense conversations between Taylor as well as his fellow aircrew , and the tower's control. Taylor did not know if the area was close to Bahama as well as Key West, and he was unsure of which direction he was facing because of a compass issue. The control tower advised Taylor that he couldn't have been located in Key West since the wind on the day didn't blow in that direction. The aircrew thought that their compass had been working. Taylor then established a course north following their compass which would have led them to Florida If they were situated in Key West. In the event that this did not work, Taylor set a course west based on their compass. This should be able to get them to Florida when the location was in Bahama. If Taylor continued on this route, it would have taken him to land prior to running out of gas.

But, at some point Taylor realized that he hadn't attempted to go to the west and was not getting enough. Then, he determined to fly toward the northeast, thinking that they might be near Key West after all. Then, the plane ran out of fuel and could have been swept into the ocean to the north of Abaco Island, and east of Florida.9

Chapter 10: Gas Explosions In Bermuda Triangle

The Bermuda Triangle is an area of the Atlantic Ocean defined roughly as the space comprising Florida, Puerto Rico, and Bermuda It is a hotspot of mystery and legend for both writers and navigators. Numerous disappearances of ships and airplanes have given credence to the mysterious elements associated with Bermuda Triangle. Bermuda Triangle. Even before the Triangle even was given a name, William Shakespeare was inspired by the tales of the Caribbean mystery, and composed the most well-known productions, "The Tempest". Despite the many years of disappearances and wrecks that have occurred in the ocean's tidal zone there is a myth and story that persists about the reason Bermuda Triangle is a place of mystery. Bermuda Triangle claims so many tragic tales. It is difficult to decide which story to believe.

4-1: Methane Gas?

A rather baffling theory suggests the geochemical effect of methane gas at the seafloor. If the soils of the seafloor change, methane gas that was trapped beneath can explode in a flash of bubbles. Many speculate that "bubbly" waters of the ocean that results from this release may lower in density and make it difficult for ships passing by to stay on the water. If the highly explosive methane gas is released into the air there is a possibility that a plane flying by could explode as a result of the collision of plane's engines and methane. This would explain why so many vessels and planes disappear without trace in the Bermuda Triangle. Unfortunately, the huge distances that methane gas has to travel from the ocean floor to the atmosphere would cast doubt on the validity in this hypothesis.

4-2 : How Do You Stay Calm During the currents?

Some believe that the history of the Bermuda Triangle's turbulent past on the treacherous Sargasso Sea that lies within the boundaries of the Triangle. The Sargasso Sea is unique because its boundaries are not defined by the land, but rather by the strong currents which are surrounding it. In the center of these currents, the calm, almost windless waters are home to dense seaweed mats that are floating. It's not surprising that even in the present, abandoned vessels are trapped by the tangled plants. There are no winds to move ships in a safe manner The Sargasso Sea has been the risk to ships that depend on force of the wind to propel them and steer. Although the Sargasso Sea might explain some of the risks ships encounter when traveling through in the Bermuda Triangle, it fails to explain the hundreds of ships and planes disappearing without trace.

4-3: Other Possibilities

The disappearances and disappearances in Bermuda Triangle Bermuda Triangle are unremarkable when the weather-related and physical issues that travelers confront in this region of ocean have been taken into consideration. The Triangle is vulnerable to hurricanes and storms which could confuse navigators and cause equipment to fail. Certain areas in the Triangle are brimming with sharp coral , which can tear holes in ships, causing their sinking. Deep trenches and pockets in the bottom of the ocean could hide the remains of wrecks which are believed to have vanished without any trace. Whatever the real cause behind these Bermuda Triangle tragedies, this area will undoubtedly be an important source of legends and intrigue for the years to in the future.

Fig . 4-1: The Bermuda Triangle

4-4: The Bermuda Triangle

Find out details concerning The Bermuda Triangle mystery with our fascinating facts, mysteries as well as theories and history. Are the reported aircraft and ship disappearances and incidents related to a supernatural power or have the stories about the Bermuda Triangle been exaggerated?

Maybe science can provide some answers. Perhaps it is possible that the Bermuda Triangle is actually no distinct from other areas of the ocean.

* Situated within the Atlantic Ocean, the Bermuda Triangle is located in between Bermuda, Puerto Rico and Florida.

*The Bermuda Triangle has long been believed to be the place in which a variety of enigmatic boat and plane accidents have been reported.

Although it is now popular to connect with the Bermuda Triangle to paranormal activity However, the majority of investigations show that poor weather or human error are more likely to be the causes.

Studies have suggested that a lot of stories of bizarre incidents within the Bermuda Triangle were exaggerated and the number of incidents occurring in the region is similar to other regions of the ocean.

Although its name may be a cause for concern however, Bermuda Triangle is not a frightful place. Bermuda Triangle is actually part of a regular sailing shipping lane that includes cruise vessels and other boats regularly traveling through the area.

Aircrafts are also prevalent within the Bermuda Triangle with both private commercial and private planes operating in the airspace.

The stories of mysterious disappearances within the Bermuda Triangle started to reach the public's attention around 1950, and have been reported on consistently since the time of publication.

Unverified explanations of supernatural origins of Bermuda Triangle incidents have included UFO-related references, and legends of the lost continent Atlantis.

Other explanations include the possibility of magnetic anomalies and pirates intentional sinkings, hurricanes gas deposits as well as rough weather, huge waves, and human mistakes.

Some of the most famous reported incidents in Bermuda Triangle Bermuda Triangle include: * The USS Cyclops and the crew of 309 disappeared after departing Barbados in 1918.

*The TBM Avenger bombers that went missing in 1945 on an exercise aircraft flight across the Atlantic.

* Douglas DC-3 aircraft containing 32 people was reported missing in the year 1958. No trace of the plane was ever located.

* A boat was discovered in 1955 , which had survived three hurricanes , however it was missing its entire crew.

Fig . 4-2: Bermuda Triangle

4 - Famous Mysterious Stories of the Bermuda Triangle

Bermuda triangle is also known also as Devil's Triangle, happens to be among the most mysterious spots on earth. The Bermuda Triangle is located off the southeast coastline of the US in the Atlantic Ocean, between Bermuda, Florida and Puerto Rico The region has been dubbed the center of mystery.

With a total area that covers 440,000 miles of sea It is the Bermuda triangle is an important shipping route with numerous vessels heading for America, Europe and the Caribbean passing through each day.

It's also due to the unfathomable effects which make it a well investigated, yet mysterious part in the surface of Earth.

Over the years, numerous planes and ships are believed to have mysteriously vanished in the area.

Additionally, the Devil's Triangle has been blamed for the disappearance of tens of thousands of people over the last years.

The phrase "Bermuda Triangle" was first utilized in the writings of Vincent Gaddis in 1964 in his piece published in Argosy magazine.

Fig . 4-3: Bermuda Triangle

The tales of the Bermuda triangle began at the time of Christopher Columbus when he was reported to have seen the flame of fire crash into the ocean in the triangle during his initial journey into New World. New World.

The mysterious behavior of the region was brought to the attention of the public at the turn of the century after the Navy cargo ship, USS Cyclops, with more than 300 persons on board, vanished within the Bermuda triangle. The most recent incident that has occurred in the region is the disappearance an aircraft with a twin engine in May of this year.

There were four passengers on board The plane disappeared from radar as it was traveling between Puerto Rico to Florida, and the debris of the plane went missing later.

4-5-1 : The most recent incident involving a ship is the sinking and destruction of a commercial vessel within the Bermuda Triangle during a deadly storm in the month of October, 2015.

The accidents, usually inexplicably, continue to happen throughout the Bermuda Triangle region, many have provided a variety of explanations to the mystery that lies that lies behind the accidents.

The significance of paranormal activity and the existence of aliens has been strongly claimed from those that believe that something unusual is occurring, but scientists have often disagree, and offered rational explanations for the phenomena.

There are a few scientific theories that have been proposed. explanations, the most popular is electromagnetic interference theory which causes compass issues.

The theory suggests that there's a powerful pull of the earth's magnetic field which can redirect the compass as well as other high-tech equipment, and prevents them to follow their planned route through the oceans.

Although, as no one theory has a solid explanation, many people believe that there is nothing odd about the region, since the majority of the incidents were incorrectly described or fictionalized versions of the events.

4-5-2 : Despite the fact that there is no established theory as to the precise cause that is the Bermuda Triangle, the accidents continue to occur each year in the region.

The legends surrounding the Bermuda Triangle consists of a many of the mysterious disappearances of vessels operating in the region, and many remain at the least clueless. Here's a list of the most famous stories of disappearance or inexplicably unsolved mysteries surrounding ship wrecks that occurred in the Devil's Triangle.

4-6): Mary Celeste

One of the most enigmatic tales of shipwrecks, this ship has a story that is its own. Although it was found floating in another location in the Atlantic Ocean, the connection to the Bermuda triangle had been in the search for an solution to the mystery of the ship's fate.

Found on December 4, 1872, with everything on the spot, except for the entire crew. The ship was discovered stranded in the ocean days following it's journey to New York to Genoa, Italy.

Seven crew members as well as captain Benjamin Briggs, his wife and their 2-year-old daughter were aboard the ship, packed with raw alcohol.

Fig . 4-4: Bermuda Triangle

4-7 : Famous Bermuda Triangle Stories

Then, just a few days later when a approaching British ship named Dei Gratia found Mary Celeste with a partial sail in the Atlantic near the Azores Islands the ship was completely unmanned without a crew in the Azores Islands as well as the lifeboat missing.

It was also discovered that nine barrels of the container were unfilled and there was also a knife on the deck. The identity of the persons who were aboard the vessel or in the lifeboat that went missing has been discovered.

The studies of the ship eliminated an attack by pirates as all the items on the vessel including the alcohol barrels it was carrying as well as the crew's valuable possessions were safe.

Theories about the mystery surrounding Mary Celeste's disappearance Mary Celeste also included the possibilities of a conspiracy of criminals as well as alien abductions or even an attack by an enormous Squid. The possibility of natural disaster was also mentioned. A number of people suggested an undersea earthquake to cause the disaster, while a small number suggested an accidental foraying of the vessel to Bermuda Triangle. Bermuda Triangle.

But, even if these ideas seem plausible however, they aren't in the right place. For instance how could a experienced crew on a great weather day, and with their vessel completely unharmed, leave it , only to never return again?

4-8 : Ellen Austin

It's an unsettling triangle mystery connected with an American White Oak sailing vessel Ellen Austin. It was in 1881 that the 210 foot length Ellen Austin was going to New York from London when she discovered a decrepit structure close to the Bermuda Triangle. Everything was in order as the unidentified schooner sailed to the north of Sargasso Sea, however, the missing crew was not there.

Captain Baker of the Ellen Austin asked to observe the abandoned vessel for two days in order to make sure that the ship isn't being used as an opportunity to trap. After two days of no reply from the vessel Captain Baker stepped inside the ship's abandoned location together with his crew and found the carefully packed shipment but there was no sign or sign of the crew.

To bring it back together along with Ellen Austin, the captain set up a prize crew on the vessel, and set it to sail in tandem. But after two days of sailing in tranquil waters, a squall divided the paths of two ships, after which the abandoned vessel disappeared.

A few days after the storm, as per the reports Captain Baker's watchdog could see the ship through his eye but then see the ship wandering off aimlessly again. After several hours of hard work, Ellen Austin could catch up to the vessel.

However, it was odd that there was no one aboard. But, another version of the story suggests that there was a another attempt made by Baker to return her to shore, but that failed with the same fate as Ellen Austin before abandoning the cursed vessel.

There are reports that suggest the abandoned structure was once discovered, but this time with an entirely different crew from the prize crew, which was placed upon it by Ellen Austin.

The disappearance of the ship, its reappearance as well as the crew's disappearance is a fascinating story. It's more like an unsolved mystery that lies within the Bermuda triangle which has never been solved any time soon.

4-9: USS Cyclops

In the event of their disappearance, USS Cyclops the largest of the Navy's largest fuel vessels, is the most significant loss of lives in the history of the US Navy in a single incident.

In the month of March 1918, this huge ship set sail across Brazil in the direction of Baltimore in the Bermuda region. It was carrying 10,800 tonnes of manganese ore, with around 309 people on board. The ship set off on a good day, the ship's initial and sole message stated there was no issue.

The ship, however, was never seen for the next few years. An exhaustive investigation of the area was conducted but nothing was discovered. There is no trace of the ship or crew members have been ever discovered.

The Captain on the USS Cyclops never sent a distress signal and no person aboard was able to respond to radio messages from other vessels nearby.

The naval investigators were unable to determine a definitive motive for the disappearance even although there were a variety of theories suggesting different causes.

In the wake of the mystery surrounding its disappearance, Cyclops has become part of the list of over 100 planes and ships to disappear in bizarre conditions during the Bermuda triangle.

4-10: Carroll A. Deering

Carroll A. Deering, an schooner commercial with five masts, is among the most popular maritime mysteries in the 20th century because of the mystery surrounding the ship's abandonment.

Conclusion

According to numerous studies conducted by scientists that have found that 129 planes disappeared from the Bermuda Triangle between 1945 and the year 2008. The frequency of paranormal activity has decreased in the Triangle over the past few years, and some researchers are asking whether the anomaly might have moved in a different direction, with some incidents near those in the Bermuda Triangle region. The book provides an overview of the theories, background and disappearances that have occurred in this mysterious region. There is no convincing scientific proof with absolute certainty to establish whether that Bermuda Triangle is real or not. Bermuda Triangle is fact or fiction. The absence of documented physical evidence supports the idea of it is not a fact or fiction. Bermuda Triangle will remain one of the biggest mysteries that remain unsolved and legends of all time.

www.ingramcontent.com/pod-product-compliance
Lightning Source LLC
Chambersburg PA
CBHW050400120526
44590CB00015B/1770